Physics of Animation

Are you an animator looking to bring your creations to life with a touch of realism? Or perhaps a game developer seeking to deepen your understanding of the forces that govern movement? In *Physics of Animation*, you'll find a comprehensive guide that bridges the gap between the art of animation and the science of physics. Drawing from seminal works like *The Animator's Survival Kit* and *The Illusion of Life*, as well as the wisdom of legendary physicists and mathematicians like Isaac Newton, Albert Einstein, Walter Lewin, and David Sang, this book provides a unique perspective on the principles that make animation believable. Wilson Labriola is a seasoned game developer and professor, who has observed firsthand the challenges many animators face due to a lack of physics knowledge. *Physics of Animation* demystifies complex concepts and presents them in an accessible and practical manner. With clear explanations, vivid illustrations, and easy-to-follow text, this book makes the laws of physics approachable for animators of all skill levels. Whether you're a novice or a seasoned professional, you'll find valuable insights to enhance the realism and quality of your animations.

Wilson Labriola is an animator and educator. As a game developer, he has worked on titles such as *Grand Theft Auto*, *Star Wars: Jedi Survivor*, *FarCry 6*, *Bioshock 4*, *Watchdogs: Legion* and the upcoming *Fable* game.

Physics of Animation

Wilson Labriola

CRC Press
Taylor & Francis Group
Boca Raton London New York

CRC Press is an imprint of the
Taylor & Francis Group, an **informa** business

Designed cover image: Wilson Labriola

First edition published 2027
by CRC Press
2385 NW Executive Center Drive, Suite 320, Boca Raton FL 33431

and by CRC Press
4 Park Square, Milton Park, Abingdon, Oxon, OX14 4RN

CRC Press is an imprint of Taylor & Francis Group, LLC

ISBN: 9781041079156 (hbk)
ISBN: 9781041079149 (pbk)
ISBN: 9781003642824 (ebk)

DOI: 10.1201/9781003642824

Typeset in Times
by codeMantra

Contents

Acknowledgements

From the moment my animation journey as a student began, I never would have pictured where my career would take me. Today, I am developing games I once played and never imagined I would be part of. While game development is my full-time job, I also work as a professor, teaching future animators and watching them achieve great things. To be honest, I sometimes can't believe that this is what I do for a living; it feels surreal.

Throughout my career, I have observed that many of the terms used in animation are concepts already established in physics.

Despite this, as I progressed through my career, I realized that many artists dislike discussing math, physics, and the technical aspects of the craft. Unfortunately, not discussing these aspects when talking about art and animation limits the artist's potential. As Oscar Wilde once said, "Art imitates life."[1] It was noticing this limitation that led me to realize how closely related animation and physics are, yet many people disregard this relationship.

I believe that, by design, we humans are curious creatures, and discovering "the why" is part of our nature. I started this book with the goal of combining my love for animation and science, and of providing you, the reader, with answers to why things happen the way they do.

As my animation research deepened over the years and my questions piled up, I began seeking answers outside the animation world. Instead, I looked at our world and the universe. Eventually, I realized that some aspects of animation reminded me of my high school physics classes. The more I learned, the clearer it became that my industry colleagues and high school science teachers were saying the same thing in different words.

Fortunately, I have surrounded myself with great people who can navigate both realms and mentor me through my career, and I encourage any budding animators to do the same. I shifted my focus to understand how and why things move and behave the way they do, and went beyond a handful of the same books and training that most people around me suggested, on my journey of personal growth.

For instance, if you observe the work of artists like Leonardo Da Vinci, Michelangelo, Raffaello, and many others, the study and execution of human anatomy, proportions, geometry, and composition are heavily explored. How can we consider anatomy but disregard physics when talking about animation? The answer is, we cannot.

Shortly after landing my first job in the industry, I received an offer to teach animation at a college. This position allowed me to learn as much as I taught and to implement the ideas I explored in this book.

Curiosity has led me to work on this passion project you have in your hands, and I dedicate this book to it.

> Remember to look up at the stars and not down at your feet. Try to make sense of what you see and wonder about what makes the universe exist. Be curious. And however difficult life may seem, there is always something you can do and succeed at. It matters that you don't just give up.
>
> *–Stephen Hawking, 2018*

I want to thank my wife and best friend, Lorna, for her support over these years and for being the number one believer that I could write this book. But not only that, I thank you for the hours of honest feedback and revisions; this book is much more interesting because of you.

My friends, Viss and Michael, your regular check-ups on the progress of this book provided the extra motivation I needed to keep going. Thank you for believing I could make this happen.

To my publisher, CRC Press, and the editorial team, Sean and Alyss, I want to express my gratitude for believing in this project. I cannot imagine how far I could have come writing this book without your support.

Finally, this book would never have been written if it weren't for the amazing people and artists I've had the pleasure to meet throughout my life and career, whom I can't name here, or it would be like a list of movie credits. Thank you for your mentoring and friendship.

NOTE

1 Oscar Wilde, *The Decay of Lying* (1889).

REFERENCE

Stephen Hawking (2018). 'Remember to look up at the stars': The best Stephen Hawking quotes. https://www.theguardian.com/science/2018/mar/14/best-stephen-hawking-quotes-quotations

Gravity

1

My reason for starting this book with gravity is that, despite perhaps not fully understanding its fundamental nature, we're all aware that it is present and acting upon us at all times.

As much as we acknowledge and experience gravity as a natural phenomenon, either through Isaac Newton's Law of Universal Gravitation or Albert Einstein's Theory of General Relativity, gravity is so deeply embedded in our daily lives that we tend to ignore it most of the time, only remembering when our phones are diving straight to our toes.

For that reason, inexperienced animators often disregard gravity's effects. This is not intentional. Their focus is on delivering great poses and performances. In order to achieve this, however, fundamental concepts must not be overlooked. The reason I wrote this book is to help you think about all possible scenarios and solutions for your next animations.

Gravity is a natural phenomenon described by Isaac Newton as a force that attracts objects and, according to Albert Einstein, as a curvature of spacetime and not a force per se. Both models are relevant for science, and neither cancels the other. While we will examine both models in this book, it is important for the animator to understand that Newton's Universal Gravitation is easier to apply when creating animations. Simply put, instead of a falling object remaining in place as the ground moves up, as general relativity states, the object falls onto the ground, as Newton suggests. This is because we tend to animate characters and objects more often than we animate the environment. For that reason, my examples will focus more on Newton's theory of gravity.

When animating, it's essential to consider how gravity affects your characters and objects. The effects of gravity in your animation can determine how immersive and realistic the experience will be for your audience. Failing to deliver the appropriate and consistent sense of weight due to gravity creates a half-baked shot, and your audience will feel that something is not right, even if they can't precisely explain what. This creates an interruption in the flow and continuity, taking your audience out of the experience and leading them to miss important details in the story.

Before you jump into your animation, take a second to consider and reflect on where your scene takes place. For the examples below, I'll be using Earth as a reference since it's a place we're all familiar with—and gravity is constantly at work here, even if you don't always notice it.

With that, I will ask the first of many questions in this book for you to ponder. Does setting matter?

DOI: 10.1201/9781003642824-1

In my opinion, yes!

Because everything on Earth is constantly being pulled towards its centre by gravity, we're all in a constant battle against it to stay upright, and this struggle is something you need to keep in mind when animating.

In animation, the silhouette is a fundamental principle to keep in mind. The image shown in Figure 1.1 is one example of defining gravity through that; let's analyse it.

FIGURE 1.1 Silhouettes of an elder and a young person.

Looking at the silhouettes above, you can easily spot who is the younger person, and why is that?

The spine of an older person tends to curve slightly in a C shape compared to the upright posture of a much younger person. An older adult will have years ahead of gravity compressing their joints and discs until the body slowly surrenders to the unyielding power of gravity acting upon us all.

This height difference is most noticeable when comparing an elder and a younger person; however, gravity is so powerful that we also tend to shrink slightly even as the day progresses. This is because most of the time, we're standing or sitting, which compresses our spine and makes us shorter. When we lie down horizontally, the spine decompresses from the force that was pulling us down.

In space, the difference can be greater than on Earth. An astronaut can grow by a couple of centimetres without gravity compressing their joints. Imagine that, next time someone asks your height if you overshot it by 2 cm, maybe even more, you're just saying your space height and not technically lying about it.

A great starting point for every animator is the classic bouncing ball. It teaches us the basics of timing, squash and stretch, spacing, and hanging time—all of which are tied to the effects of gravity. Once you master these core concepts, you can animate about anything with a sense of weight and realism.

Let me break this down for you:

A ball can't just start moving from its resting position—it needs a starting force to get it going. This is where Newton's laws of motion come into play. Without an external force, like a throw, a kick, or maybe even the wind, the ball will stay still, stuck in inertia, which we will discuss in Chapter 3.

Let's imagine the ball is held in your hand and then dropped, with no extra force applied—just released. In this case, gravity will take over, and the ball will begin descending towards the centre of the Earth until it reaches the ground or an obstacle along the way.

As the ball falls, it will start slowly but gradually pick up speed. It will continue to accelerate until one of the following two things happens:

Scenario A: The ball reaches terminal velocity. This is the maximum speed it can achieve due to air resistance pushing against it—more in Chapter 2. At this point, the force of gravity pulling the ball downwards is balanced by the air resistance pushing it upwards. The ball will continue falling at this constant speed. It's important to note that terminal velocity affects everything in free-fall.

Scenario B: The ball's descent is interrupted. That could be a surface, like the ground, or an object. If the ball interacts with an object of greater mass, the energy is transferred back, causing it to bounce. The direction and bounce are correlated to the ball's trajectory and the shape and composition of the surface it contacts.

The moment the ball begins its free-fall, there's a brief moment we call "hanging time." For brief moment the ball seems to hang motionless in the air. Then, gravity takes over, and the ball starts its downward journey – Is important to note that the acceleration at which objects fall due to gravity is $9.8 m/s^2$ when disregarding air resistance. The ball isn't yet falling at a fast or constant speed; it's just beginning its descent. The ball would need to fall from a great height to achieve terminal velocity.

Keep in mind that the speed of the fall and the altitude needed to reach terminal velocity will vary depending on the mass and shape of the object. A heavier or more aerodynamic object might fall differently than a lighter or less streamlined object.

As the ball continues to fall, it gradually picks up speed. When it finally hits a surface, the ball will deform upon impact—a result of the force of the collision. This deformation is an important part of how objects interact, so keep it in mind when animating movements like this. We will dive into deformation in Chapter 10.

In either scenario, the ball's motion results directly from gravity, air resistance, and external factors (Figure 1.2).

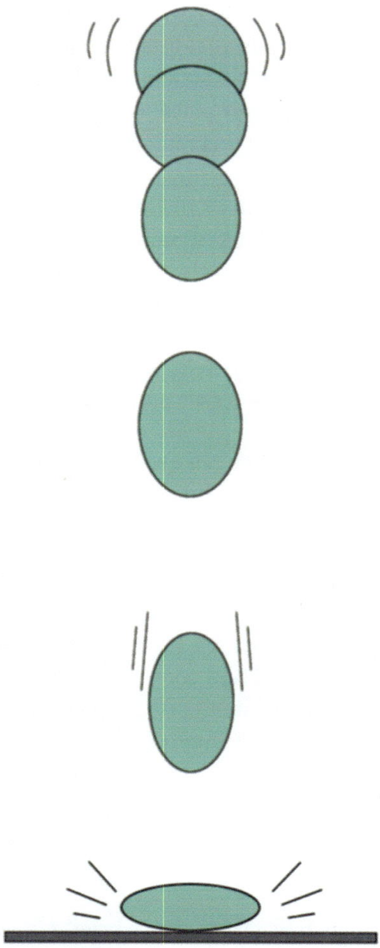

FIGURE 1.2 Image of a ball falling.

As you can imagine, when the ball hits the surface, it bounces and is projected away from it. The ball will bounce back up in this scenario since I am referencing a flat surface. The height the ball reaches after each bounce depends on a mix of factors: the force of the impact, its speed, shape, and material.

If the ball is made from a material with a mass that allows it to bounce, its upward motion will mirror its downward fall. In those first moments of rising, it behaves much like it did when it dropped, but now it's heading back up.

When the ball hits the surface, the energy from the collision, the force of gravity, and the ball's material all work together. This energy spreads out in all directions, causing the ball to deform. But once the ball reaches its limit, with nowhere else for the energy to go, it forces it to rebound upwards.

The ball's speed and energy peak as it rises during each bounce. This is when the ball has the most energy—thanks to the combination of the force of the impact and the material it's made from—all working in unison to push it back into the air.

However, even though the object's goal is to stay in a state of motion, when we discuss inertia in Chapter 3, each bounce causes the ball to lose some energy as gravity always acts against it, pulling it back towards the ground and slowing it down. As a result, the ball will eventually lose enough energy to no longer reach the same height as before (Figure 1.3).

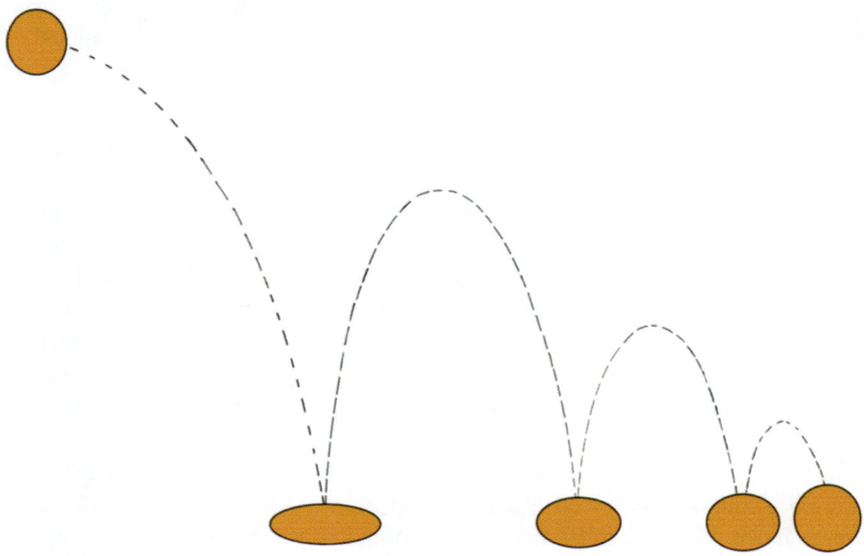

FIGURE 1.3 Image of a bouncing ball losing energy.

Let's take the same concept of a bouncing ball and apply it to a person jumping. Unlike the ball, we do not need a push to start the motion—we have muscles, bones, joints, and brains working together to get us moving. However, we need to generate power to jump higher, just like the ball does when it compresses. So, we crouch, bending our knees to act like a spring.

Once we push off the ground and lose contact with the surface, we launch ourselves into the air, trying to defy gravity. But, just like the ball, gravity will eventually pull us back down. As we reach the highest point of our jump, we start to lose acceleration, and for a split second, we almost seem to hang in the air until gravity pulls us back into reality and proves that we can't just break the gravitational pull with sheer will and knees.

From there, we start the descent slowly and pick up speed as we fall. The same principles that govern a bouncing ball apply to us. Gravity constantly acts on everything, shaping how things move, whether a ball or a person (Figure 1.4).

FIGURE 1.4 Image of a person jumping.

Now that you have a good grasp of how a bouncing ball and a person jumping work, let's change the scenario and use a rocket as an example:

Because of its mass, material, and shape, a rocket needs a significant push to overcome gravity's pull. This is where fuel comes in. During the countdown, the rocket burns most of its fuel, using up an enormous amount of energy to lift off the tons of metal, cargo, and also fuel, since moving any object from a state of rest requires much more energy. As the rocket ascends and leaves the atmosphere, its acceleration increases, but things change once it reaches the vacuum of space. In space, there's very little resistance, so the rocket needs much less fuel to keep moving forward (Vacuum & Space: Chapter 2).

This is also one of the reasons scientists, governments, and entrepreneurs are so interested in building bases on the Moon and Mars. The gravitational pull on these bodies is much weaker than Earth's, so launching a rocket from there requires far less fuel—making space exploration more affordable.

In this rocket scenario, the pacing and timing differ from a person or creature jumping. The rocket starts slowly, gradually picking up speed as it rises. It's a slow build, but it can move much more efficiently once it's out of the atmosphere (Figure 1.5).

1.1 LAW OF UNIVERSAL GRAVITATION

The universal law of gravitation states that every object with mass exerts gravity on every other object. The larger an object's mass, the stronger its gravitational pull.

This means that, technically, everybody—whether it's a planet, a rock, or even you—pulls on other bodies. But when compared to the massive force of a planet like Earth, the gravitational pull of smaller objects becomes insignificant.

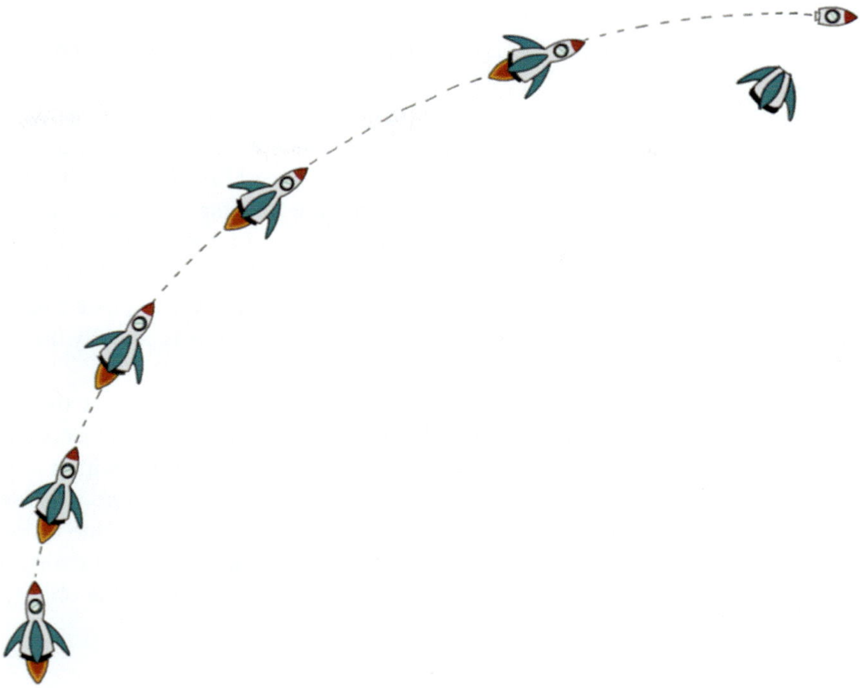

FIGURE 1.5 Image of a rocket launching and its trajectory.

Here's a fun and random thought: imagine an astronaut stranded in space with a marble floating nearby. Since the astronaut carries more mass than a marble, the astronaut exerts a gravitational pull on the object. Over time, the marble would slowly drift towards them.

Now, consider why the moon doesn't crash into Earth. It's because the moon's gravity affects Earth's gravity, and Earth's gravity affects the moon. This mutual attraction is what causes the tides. Earth's gravity keeps the moon in orbit, preventing it from falling into us.

Gravity, like the air, is so deeply embedded in our lives, though blind to our eyes, that we often do not think about it. For this reason, we tend to ignore it when animating, but understanding it can be useful, especially if you ever find yourself developing a story or working on a specific task heavily focused on gravity.

1.2 THEORY OF GENERAL RELATIVITY

Einstein's theory of general relativity[1] offers a very interesting perspective on gravity, and I personally think it is worth including a passage about it in this book. The idea from the theory of general relativity is that, instead of gravity being an invisible force of attraction between objects, as the story of the apple falling from a tree tells us, in this scenario, the apple is not the one falling from a tree, but the planet moving upwards to encounter the apple.

Einstein describes gravity as curvature in spacetime caused by an object's mass and energy, and the "attraction" results from objects moving through space along this path, called geodesics. A really interesting example is a world map. When viewed flat, drawing straight vertical and horizontal lines along the 2D map will make them look straight. However, if you take this map and wrap it around a sphere, those lines will form curves in their paths, and since the universe is not flat, but curved, as Einstein suggests, gravity is not a force at all. So, next time you wonder why a plane trajectory appears curved or seems to take a longer route, remember that this is actually the shortest distance when considering the planet's curvature.

A common misconception in the theory of general relativity is that the fabric of space is flat, which cannot accurately describe the trajectories that objects follow in space. However, in reality, this curvature occurs in all directions within a four-dimensional plane, with time serving as the fourth coordinate. The more massive an object is, the greater its influence on the fabric of space and time. Imagine dropping a heavy ball onto a trampoline—the fabric curves around the ball, but in reality, this effect stretches out in every direction, not just one. The more massive the object, the more dramatic the curvature it creates (Figures 1.6 and 1.7).

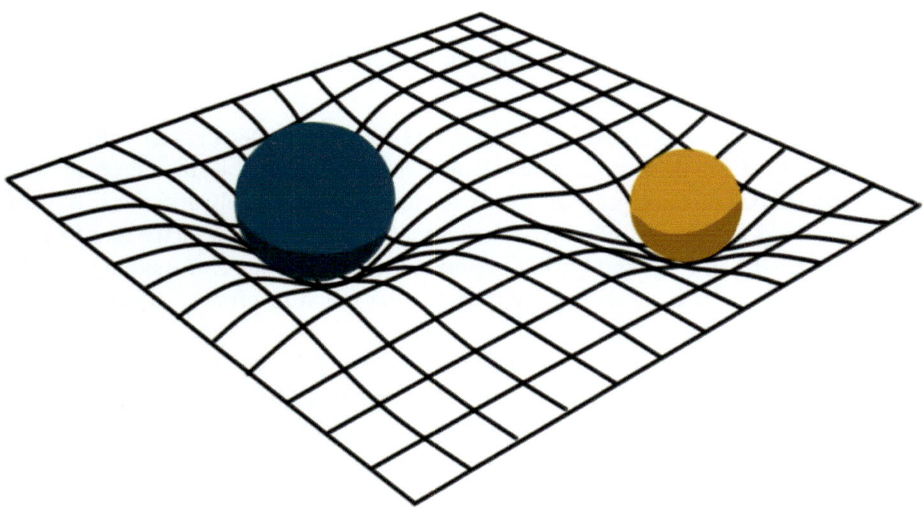

FIGURE 1.6 Image of the fabric of space warped by masses.

As important and relevant as Einstein's theory of general relativity is for physics and our understanding of the universe, in practical terms for animation, it is not something you'll need to think about or apply as often as the other knowledge shared in this book. However, I encourage you to explore more examples if this is something you are curious about.

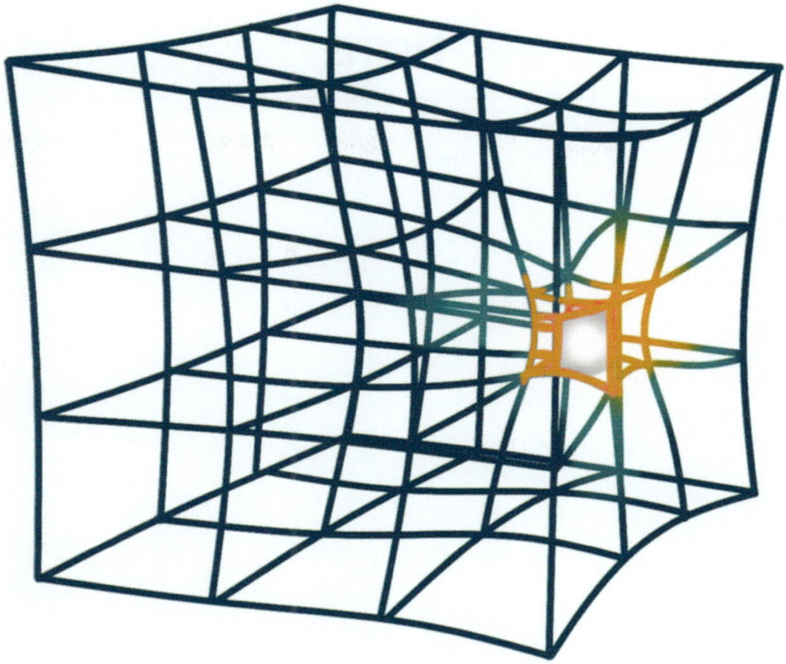

FIGURE 1.7 3D image of the fabric of space warped by a body.

CHAPTER SUMMARY

- Gravity is a natural phenomenon, and the two models used to describe it are the Law of Universal Gravitation and the Theory of General Relativity.
- Considering how gravity behaves and the effects in the world being created, will make the animation and story believable.
- Make sure to have a setting before starting your next animation.
- The bouncing ball animation is the foundation for everything else that lands from a free-fall.
- Consider how the falling object's trajectory, its composition, and the surface interacting with it influence the reaction force and final trajectory.
- The Law of Universal Gravitation, by Isaac Newton, states that every object with mass exerts gravity on every other object.
- The Theory of General Relativity observes gravity as a curvature of space and time.

NOTE

1 Albert Einstein, *The Foundation of the General Theory of Relativity* (1916) and *Relativity: The Special and General Theory* (1920).

Air Resistance

2

If you've ever played with a Frisbee, you might have noticed that it glides smoothly through the air, but at some point, it starts to lose momentum until it gently lands. The reason it glides easily through the air is its shape, weight, acceleration, and angle of attack. The frisbee functions much like an aircraft wing, which is designed to improve airflow along the curved top, creating lower pressure. As the air travels from the flatter area beneath, it builds pressure, increasing lift.

On the other hand, F1 cars are designed to do the opposite. They are designed to create airflow that generates downward force, pressing the car onto the track. This is achieved, simply speaking, by flipping their rear and front wings. The airflow helps keep the car safely planted at high speeds.

As you can see, the design and positioning of objects that are made to move through air must follow certain principles to achieve optimal aerodynamics. This applies not only to frisbees, airplanes, or F1 cars, but to all objects and living things. It is important therefore to carefully plan for air resistance, or drag, when animating (Figure 2.1).

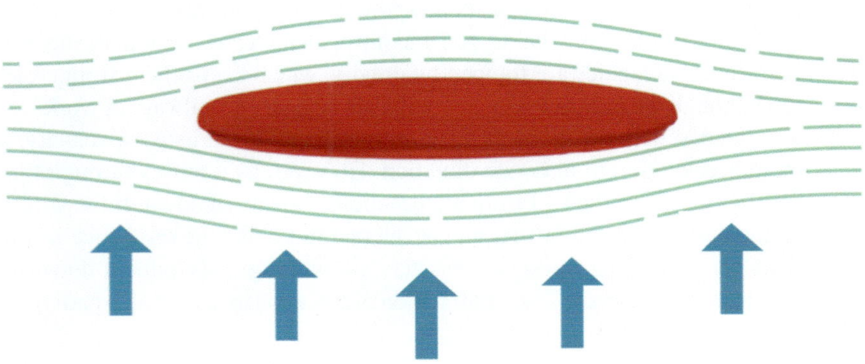

FIGURE 2.1 Image of a frisbee in motion with air resistance around it.

It is easy to think that air resistance affects only flying objects; however, its effects can be observed in humans as well.

I'm sure that right now your brain is creating several scenarios in which air resistance affects us, probably even thinking about how to apply it in your next animation. If not, I will show a few examples you've probably experienced.

DOI: 10.1201/9781003642824-2

During a walk, we usually don't notice how much air resistance affects us because we can generate enough force to cut through the air easily. This is because the oxygen and nitrogen molecules are extremely light, causing less resistance than our bodies do. However, when these molecules move at very high speeds, generating wind, we encounter much greater resistance, which can sometimes be enough to carry us along with almost everything that is in contact with it.

Another example you may have seen or tried is sticking your arm out the window of a moving car against the wind. Although I don't recommend it for safety reasons, it is another way to experience how air resistance works in real life. By spreading the fingers wide with an open palm, the air molecules hit the flat surface of the hand like a punch, since they have to travel across the entire surface to exit on the other side as more air contacts the hand. However, by keeping the fingers close together like a spearhead, the air flows much more smoothly through the hand, creating less resistance.

As observed, air resistance affects every moving thing; however, the result of this force depends on the subject's shape, mass, composition, and acceleration.

Now that you better understand gravity and its impact on your scenes, let's add another layer to the mix—air resistance. This force plays a key role in determining how objects move, and understanding it will enable you to create more realistic animations.

2.1 AIR RESISTANCE (DRAG)

Imagine throwing a baseball. You know it will eventually fall to the ground because gravity is pulling it down. But there's another force at play—air resistance.

Air resistance results from the oxygen and nitrogen molecules that make up Earth's atmosphere. These molecules are trapped by gravity, which keeps them from escaping into space. Although we may not notice it daily, air resistance is always at work.

Back to the baseball, the moment it leaves your hand, it's at its peak velocity, with its maximum acceleration in only one direction. However, as it moves through the air, the same pushes it against the ball from all directions, slowing it down. If the wind is at your back, the ball will travel farther and accelerate more, but air resistance is always present. This constant force works against the ball, while gravity pulls it downwards, creating an arc in its trajectory. The combination of forces shapes the ball's path through the air (Figure 2.2).

FIGURE 2.2 Image of a baseball experiencing air resistance.

Now, instead of a ball, picture throwing a sheet of paper. What do you think is going to happen?

The paper composition is not only light, but its large and with a flat surface area, lacking in a shape that can create lift, as discussed earlier, making it more susceptible to air resistance due to the increased number of air molecules that it will come into contact with, slowing it down faster than the ball. In short, its trajectory is much shorter because of its shape, mass, and composition.

The simple act of folding the sheet into a paper plane makes the object more aerodynamic and capable of keeping lift compared to the sheet.

Finally, instead of changing the object this time. Let's change the scene. Imagine throwing a ball underwater. In this new environment, the ball will move much more slowly because water particles are packed closer together than in air, leading to increased friction as the ball moves.

For the animator, it is vital to understand not only the characters and objects but also the environment where the animation occurs. Considering what surrounds the character and how everything connects is the first step before gathering references. For example, when working with projectiles, the animator should think about the trajectory, shape, acceleration, mass, and composition. Then, the angle of attack must be considered, whether the object is moving under its own propulsion or being launched by someone. This brings us to another aspect to consider: what should be done when a character throws an object? Body mechanics will influence the angle at which the object travels, but that's not all. As mentioned earlier, the body's shape and mechanics are also affected by air resistance. For that reason, the animator should consider how the character's acceleration or timing is affected by the drag force. As with projectiles, the animator needs to take into account all the factors mentioned above, as well as friction, which will be discussed in Chapter 8.

Going back to our original example of a frisbee, consider human anatomy and mechanics so that the throw feels like an extension of the disc. Precision is key, and the action must follow a few fundamental principles to achieve optimal results.

If you're like me and lack the skills to throw a Frisbee properly, you will see something different when the disc tries its best to glide smoothly. Failing to maintain the correct orientation creates turbulence on the frisbee, resulting in a less smooth glide and a shorter distance travelled. Key factors include the angle at which the disc sits before the throw, the grip, the energy transfer from the hip to wrist, and, in most cases, a proper balance.

Throwing objects will achieve optimal results in terms of speed and trajectory if the origin—our arms and hands, or our legs and feet—follows a trajectory that maintains continuity of movement from its starting point to the moment we release the object. Remember that everything in our bodies moves along an arc.

Picture someone throwing a Frisbee, and ask yourself some key questions, such as: What do you imagine the main poses will look like? Where is the energy originating from? And what trajectory do you want the disc to follow? With these questions answered and relevant references, you can start visualizing how this animation will play. In this scenario, I am using a Frisbee; however, the same questions can be asked for any other object.

There is no right or wrong way to start an animation. I find, however, if you ask the questions and develop a plan before starting, you'll be better prepared. This will likely save you a lot of time.

Let's break this example down:

The first pose: The hips control this action and drive the rotation, but the movement is not limited to the hips alone. After the hips initiate the motion, the upper body follows, delaying the core, chest, shoulders, arms, and head, which drags behind, as if going in the opposite direction of the throw. One last point many animators tend to overlook is that the hip can only rotate by a certain amount before creating strain on the joints due to anatomical limits. To compensate, we pivot on the foot to reach further. Pushing the character's rotation without pivoting the foot will make it feel broken. Consider applying the pivot while posing the character to avoid unnecessary foot slides. The planted foot cannot translate forward and sideways, and it needs to be pinned by the toes or ankle.

Having the proper pivots helps achieve a more appealing, stronger pose, pushing the character further and resulting in a snappier, more powerful animation, as the character must cover a larger distance from the origin to the destination.

The second pose is the release, where the driving force comes from a combination of the hips' acceleration and coverage from one pose to the next. In animation terms, this distance covered from one pose to another is known as spacing. When combined with timing, which is how long (in frames) each pose happens consecutively, the animator can determine how the animation will look like. The same delay on the rest of the body occurs until the character reaches the pose, known as offset. Not all limbs should move simultaneously; applying an offset will produce a more natural and believable animation.

In the middle, an in-between or breakdown pose is added, which is important for properly timing the animation. This pose in between can be adjusted to fix trajectories and poses, ease ins and outs, and give more flair to the animation (Figure 2.3).

Another important driving force is the upper body and arms working oppositely. Their work involves increasing the distance between the pose's origin and the object's release, controlling as much of the body as possible within its limitations, and determining the trajectory from start to finish and the final release point. In other words, more distance from the object will result in more energy to throw it further and faster.

Lastly, the object's trajectory: This final question is as important as the first two. The character movement driving the object must be concise, readable, and simple so that the audience can follow. Imagine watching an animation where a character is about to throw a Frisbee at a 15-degree angle, and when the disc is released, it glides at a 45-degree angle. You will know that something is not right. Or, picture a character throwing the Frisbee, and instead of a clean and simple arc, the animator adds poses in between, creating a broken trajectory. This example is very common among new animators who create in between to correct character poses or even the trajectory. The result can ultimately break the illusion they were trying to fix previously.

Inexperienced animators often overlook trajectories when working with props and characters, and I cannot stress enough the importance of this difference when using it versus not using it. Most animation software includes this feature, and it is quite easy to find and use. I recommend you start working with it and get used to it (Figure 2.4).

FIGURE 2.3 Image illustrating the body mechanics involved in throwing a Frisbee.

It is important to note that a complicated arc during a throw will result in a weak launch and trajectory. As the illustration above shows, three poses are enough to achieve a good trajectory. Extra poses and keys in between could break the trajectory, increase jitters, and delay production time with unnecessary reviews.

Now, picture a completely different environment, space. In the vacuum, where there's no air resistance, if you were to throw an object, it would just keep travelling forever unless something else, like the gravitational pull of a planet or star, pulls it in. It is a strange thought, isn't it? If you were to throw an object in space, you would also be affected by the same forces and likely spin in the opposite direction forever, since there is nothing to stop you.

In simple terms, a vacuum is very easy to explain when it comes to air resistance: It simply doesn't have air, so drag doesn't exist. However, it is more complicated than that. A vacuum is not the absence of everything. In space, gravity, light, radiation, and other forces can be present, and in some cases, gases and dust particles can also exist, though in much smaller amounts.

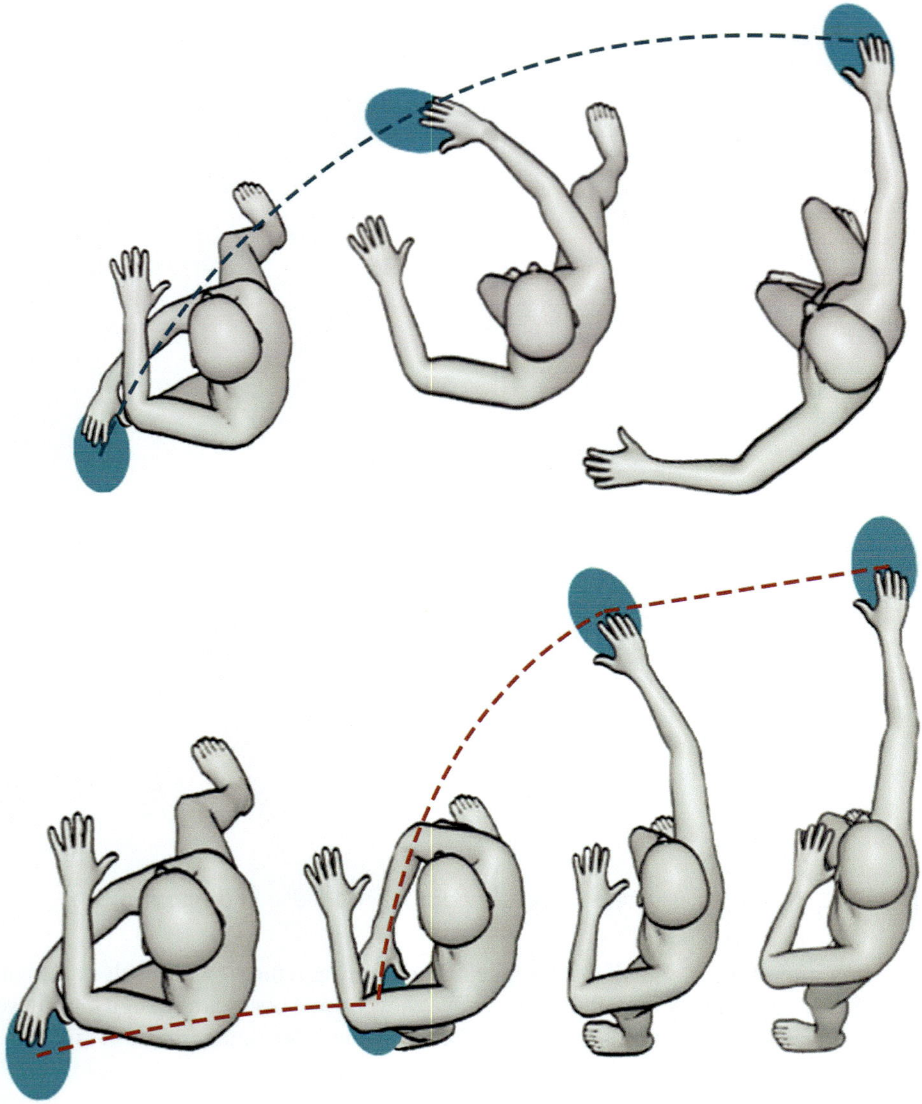

FIGURE 2.4 Images illustrating a clean and broken trajectory, caused by adding an extra pose when throwing a Frisbee.

Let's change the scene again and go to the moon, where there is gravity but no atmosphere. If you drop a hammer and a feather simultaneously, they will hit the ground at the same time. Why? Without resistance from air, gravity is the only force at work. In this case, the feather's lightness doesn't matter—it falls as quickly as the ball. This theory, first proposed by Galileo, states that the speed of falling objects depends on gravity, not mass, and was later tested and confirmed by Apollo 15 astronaut David Scott in 1971 on the surface of the moon.

When animating, remember to consider all scenarios. Observe real-life references and consider how external forces, such as gravity and air resistance, influence the objects and characters in your scene. An important factor to consider, regardless of whether it is a character or a prop, is the shape and composition, as air resistance affects objects differently depending on how they are designed, either by nature or human hand. A teardrop shape, for example, is considered the most aerodynamic shape we know. A teardrop has a very low drag coefficient compared to any other object because its shape supports airflow. The smooth front directs the air through the middle, helping to keep the object stable. At the tip, the air flows smoothly without causing turbulence. This is why sports cars, jets, and many other objects have a teardrop shape. This design not only reduces drag but also conserves energy. Even in nature, eagles, for example, and athletes in sports like cycling, curve their bodies to achieve a lower drag coefficient and use less energy.

Keep in mind details like this; it will make your animation feel real and grounded in the world you are creating.

2.2 TERMINAL VELOCITY

As the name indicates, terminal velocity is the highest speed an object can attain when falling through fluids like air or water. Additionally, gravity plays a crucial role in reaching this speed. Similar to air resistance, the shape, mass, and composition of an object influence how quickly it reaches terminal velocity.

When an object initiates its free fall, there is no air resistance. At this point, only gravity is pulling it down. As the object continues its descent, air resistance gradually increases until it balances the force of gravity. This balance between forces is the terminal velocity—the point at which it stops accelerating.

To clarify, air resistance, or drag, is the force that opposes the motion of an object through a fluid. However, as mentioned before, there are ways to observe how drag affects the falling subject.

Picture two skydivers with the same mass, both in freefall. One has their arms and legs spread wide open, while the other keeps their body compact, with arms and legs close together. Which one would reach terminal velocity first?

You're right if you guessed the first skydiver—the one keeping their arms and legs tucked in. By increasing their surface area, the spread-out skydiver builds up air resistance much faster, however at a lower speed. On the other hand, the second skydiver reaches a much higher acceleration, but not as fast terminal velocity (Figure 2.5).

Terminal velocity exists because air is a fluid, and the reason why air, like water, remains here is due to gravity. All the gases that make up the air are trapped around our planet in the atmosphere, while water, being denser than air because its molecules are closer together, is pulled by gravity into the ocean depths, the bottoms of rivers, and your coffee mug. Without gravity, the atmosphere would drift into space along with the planet's water, which is what scientists say happened to Mars. Since its gravitational

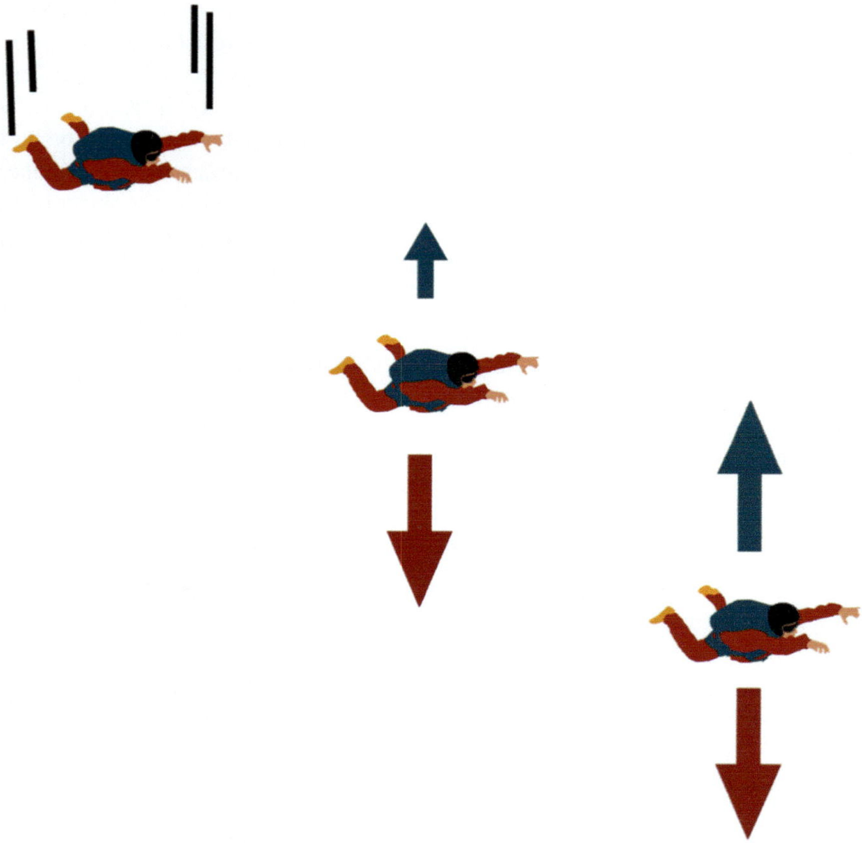

FIGURE 2.5 Image of terminal velocity on a skydiver.

pull is not strong enough and its atmosphere is very thin, the planet was not only unable to stay warm, but most or all of its liquid water was also lost, drifting into space. On the flip side, gravity can exist without an atmosphere, as we see on the moon, where there's no air, but gravity is still at work. However, terminal velocity wouldn't happen without gravity and air resistance. These two forces should work together for the terminal velocity to come into play.

Understanding the principles of air resistance is fundamental for animators when planning their story, as they will directly influence the timing and poses for both characters and objects. Integrating animation principles with physics will certainly elevate the quality of the work.

CHAPTER SUMMARY

- The subject's shape will alter how air resistance affects it.
- When a character is throwing an object, body mechanics and trajectory are essential to consider in order to achieve its full potential.
- The moving object trajectory should be clear and not deviate from its original course, unless its shape, propulsion, or external factors influence it.
- When the subject initiates their motion, either falling or any other direction, air resistance has very little effect on them.
- In the vacuum, where there is no air, objects in motion stay in motion.
- As Galileo said, "The speed of falling objects depends on gravity, not mass."
- The teardrop is the most aerodynamic shape, and its use can be seen in vehicles, in animals like the eagle, and in sports.
- Water is a fluid, so is air, and they both affect falling objects' terminal velocity.
- The shape in which a subject is made or takes will influence how quickly it reaches the terminal velocity.
- Terminal velocity only exists because we have an atmosphere to trap the air on the planet, and the reason why this happens is due to the effects of gravity.

Newton's First Law of Motion 3

At some point in your life, you might have heard that an object at rest stays at rest, and an object in motion continues in a straight line at a constant speed unless acted upon by an external force.

In *Philosophiæ Naturalis Principia Mathematica*,[1] first published in 1687, Isaac Newton introduced the first law of motion, influenced by Galileo Galilei's Law of inertia. From his experiments rolling objects down slopes, Galileo concluded that a body in motion would remain in motion unless a force acted on it, such as surface friction or air resistance, which is a form of friction called fluid friction, as the molecules of air collide with the object, creating resistance. An environment where objects are dropped with no air resistance is not naturally occurring on Earth, but there are man-made examples, such as a vacuum chamber. Since drag is always present, even when an object falls due to gravity, there is still resistance on the way to the surface it collides with. If this example involves rolling or sliding objects down a slope, surface friction also makes the task a little difficult; even the smoothest surfaces have small deformations on a microscopic level that can create resistance. In other words, it is impossible, on Earth, to see an object in motion staying in motion indefinitely.

Nowadays, we understand that friction and terrain deformation affect the ball's trajectory. However, when gravity, air resistance, and the object's mass are combined in the equation, the object will eventually stop.

For some time, I wondered how an object at rest could be explained in an animation environment, and the short answer is: You don't animate it! In other words, an object that doesn't need any movement doesn't need to be animated; the state of rest is absolute, but at the same time relative to the frame of reference of the viewer. An object at rest can be observed through camera lenses or the spectator's eyes; this is relative to what is observed. However, the camera, environment, and object could be travelling and/or spinning at high speeds, and to the viewer's eye, nothing seems to be moving. The concept of frame of reference will be further discussed in Chapter 12.

Of course, there will be cases in which you will animate objects that are at rest and some external force will make it move, a tree for example; as much as it looks at rest, external factors like a light breeze will cause the leaves to move, a strong wind shaking its branches and a hurricane pulling the entire tree off the ground. Take into consideration that every action in your animation should support the story, and that things should not just move without a reason.

DOI: 10.1201/9781003642824-3

On the other hand, inertia doesn't only mean the absence of movement or being at rest; in physics, it can also refer to uniform motion in a straight line, unless acted upon by an external force.

Uniform motion, where an object stays in motion, is very rare in animation, unless a strong reason is given for it to occur, such as exaggeration, stylization, and storytelling. These examples rarely happen when the story is grounded in realism. Forces such as gravity, friction, and air resistance will likely affect the trajectory of this object in motion, for the sake of storytelling and to keep the story grounded in reality. Not that this is a rule per se in all stories; animation can be exaggerated for the same reason mentioned above, the ultimate goal is to support the story, and if bending or breaking some rules is necessary, by all means, just keep in mind that, your animation will break the rules of physics.

A character being launched into space from a cannon, overstretching in a way that feels broken, and a baseball travelling across the planet after being hit by a baseball bat are examples of bending rules to support the story.

The first law of motion requires an understanding of the composition and external influences on objects, which are often overlooked in animation.

Picture a bowling ball resting on a surface; can you tell the main reasons why the object remains in this state? There are a few, including the laws of motion and frictional force; however, the main reason is gravity.

Gravity would continue pulling the bowling ball towards Earth's centre if it were not for the planet's crust holding it in place. Like any other object, the ball also has mass and composition sufficient to remain in place and maintain its spherical shape. An object at rest wants to stay at rest.

Object composition is important when considering the first law of motion. For the example above, I used a bowling ball, which, in its newer versions since the 1990s, is composed of materials like resin and plastic. Older versions were made of rubber, wood, and urethane (a malleable compound that falls between rubber and plastic, used in insulation, household appliances, the automotive industry, pharmaceuticals, and other applications). The reason I am describing the composition of a simple bowling ball is to exemplify how important it is for the animator to understand and research how the object will behave when interacting with the world created.

In contrast to the bowling ball, a water balloon can barely hold its shape due to its elastic composition and the water itself (more about deformation in Chapter 9).

If you roll a ball on a surface and disregard gravity, air resistance, and friction (later in this book), the ball would continue in motion indefinitely.

The same would happen in space unless an external force, such as a gravitational field or particles, is in the trajectory of the object (Figure 3.1).[2]

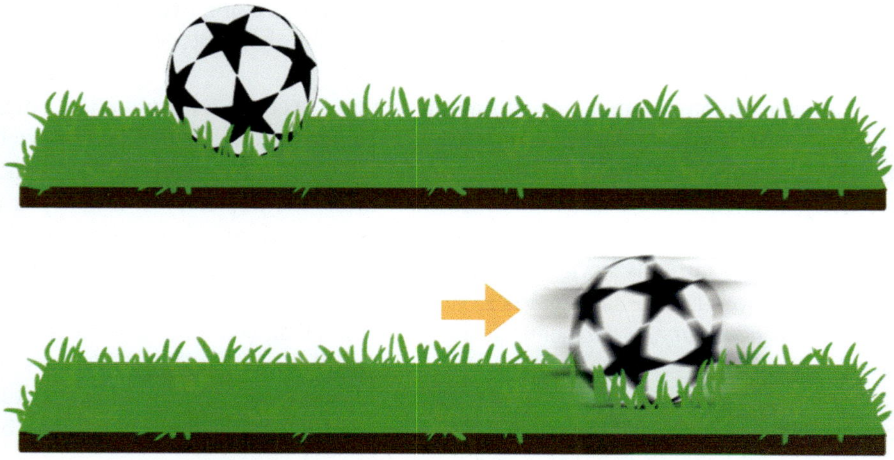

FIGURE 3.1 Image of a soccer ball at rest and in motion.

3.1 INERTIA

One thing I like to do in class with my students is the classic "bouncing ball" exercise. For this animation, I like to have the students creating a simple environment for the ball to interact with. I leave it up to them to decide how the set will be built, allowing their creativity to spark, and each one ends up with a different result. This is an exercise not only for them but also for me, since each environment will determine how the ball behaves in it, and it is great for all of us to imagine different scenarios. This assignment aims to improve timing, spacing, squash, and stretch. Still, that is not all. The idea of having them create an environment is also to think of a trigger as a starting point for the animation, so the ball does not simply drop from the middle of the screen without a reason. This could seem unnecessary, but from the standpoint of the first law of motion, this is how it should happen; an object cannot start its motion without influences. The results are impressive! I have seen trapdoors, slopes, and all sorts of shapes. Different environments for a simple exercise, such as a bouncing ball, create remarkably unique results and prompt students to consider how the environment affects animated objects and characters.

In simpler terms, this means that inanimate objects in your animation cannot begin moving from rest without an external force. Something must initiate its motion.

It might seem like a basic idea, but you'd be surprised how many animators overlook this fundamental concept at the start of their animation career. It is all too easy to get caught up in more complicated techniques, but understanding the basics of animation and physics is crucial for making progress and building the foundations that any animator should have. Mastering these fundamentals is the key to tackling more complex animations down the road.

Imagine you have an evenly shaped, perfectly balanced object sitting on a stable surface, such as a well-built table, not a wobbly, half-finished project that I would probably do quickly so I could go play some video games. When you place this object on the table, it takes a few milliseconds—or even seconds—to settle. This is due to the object being in motion as your hand brings it towards the table. Of course, the object's shape can also determine how long or if there will be settling. Once it's in place and no external force is acting on it, the object will stay there, unmoving, until the nature of the object causes it to decay. And that could take hundreds, even thousands, of years.

In this example, I'm considering two forces: friction and gravity, which are the forces acting upon all objects on this planet. As you know, gravity will pull the object onto the table due to the object's weight. Next, friction acts in two directions: the table pushes the ball up to keep it in place, and the ball pushes the table down, creating microscopic connections that allow it to remain stationary if no other external influences affect it. You can also observe this last example when discussing the third law of motion.

Have you ever noticed that when objects are dropped, thrown, or when they fall, they don't stop immediately; there is some oscillation before they come to a complete stop? This results from the object's mass and velocity interacting oppositely with external factors, such as friction, gravity, and air resistance.

In other words, imagine a rolling ball coming to a stop; the ball will not simply stop but will wiggle for some short period before it does. Now, from this generic example, start adding factors like the ball's mass, the velocity as it was rolled, the surface of the terrain, the wind, and, of course, gravity.

Acceleration and mass will dictate the momentum carried by the ball; a wrecking ball, such as the ones used in construction to demolish buildings, will carry a massive amount of momentum if rolled downhill, making it nearly unstoppable. On the other hand, a volleyball could be easily stopped if it is going downhill.

The surface the object is rolling on influences its momentum and how fast or slow it will swing before it comes to a stop. If two balls, carrying the same mass and acceleration, are rolled through tiles and grass, the result will differ. The tile surface is much smoother and solid compared to grass, which creates more friction on the object due to its irregularities and flexibility.

One more crucial factor is the shape of the object. A ball with a smooth surface will roll when pushed much more than a cube, which, depending on the acceleration and mass, might not even move at all; it might drift a little, but that is it. A ball, compared to a cube, has fewer contact points and less balance. On the other hand, a cube is very balanced and has a larger surface area with more contact points, resulting in better friction.

Now, why does the object oscillate? The first law of motion says that an object stays in motion unless it is affected by an external force. Taking this into consideration, the object wants to move indefinitely. However, gravity, friction, air resistance, and any other force will work against the object to stop it. Therefore, the oscillation occurs because the objects cannot transition from x acceleration to zero without being forced to do so. The wiggle before the object stops is the momentum carried by the object's acceleration and mass fighting against all the other external factors, and trying to find a balance to settle.

Now, let's say an earthquake occurs. What will happen to the object sitting on the table? Well, that depends. The strength of the earthquake, the stability of the building, the sturdiness of the table, and the mass and shape of the object—all of these factors come into play. As an animator, you should determine how each element influences the outcome, aiming to create the desired effect in your animation and, as always, to ask the right questions.

Let me share a story about one of my students that exemplifies an essential lesson in animation. She's an incredibly talented and creative animator, but she made a fundamental mistake that's easy to overlook in one of her pieces. The scene featured a tiger trapped in a circus cage, desperately trying to break free. You know the kind of cage I'm talking about—the one with heavy bars and wheels. It was a great animation, but something was missing.

When I asked her if she had planned to animate the cage, she paused as if struck by a realization. It was as if a light bulb went off. She hadn't thought about the cage interacting with the tiger's movements, but she understood how it would bring the animation to life once she did. That simple addition—the cage responding to the tiger's struggle—would add so much energy to the shot, which it did after this little detail was added.

This moment drives a key point about animation: the small, seemingly insignificant details often make a significant impact. A prop interacting with the character, like a very simple action of sitting on a chair and having the same reaction to the character's weight, even if just a bit. Simple, but planned movements can give the shot a sense of realism and motion. It's a sign of a true animator's eye when they notice those little things that make everything feel more alive.

3.2 OBJECTS IN MOTION STAY IN MOTION

And at a constant speed and on a straight line unless acted upon by an external force.

But in a practical context, this can be confusing. You might be thinking, "If I animate someone kicking a soccer ball or throwing a baseball, are you telling me that they won't stop and keep moving in a straight line forever?"

The answer is no, well, maybe, depending on the specific setting. When you kick a ball, the forward force moves at maximum speed. This happens because, at that moment, the leg force, in addition to the support foot using friction to remain stable, the hip to drive the force, the arms and torso for balance, are greater than the ball's mass. When this happens, the other external forces acting on the object are zero, but things change as soon as it starts rolling on the ground or is launched into the air. Friction, which we'll dive into more later in the book, will oppose the force of the ball moving forward, and finally, gravity, as you know, will pull the ball towards the ground. As these forces work together, the ball eventually loses all its energy and comes to a stop, succumbing to inertia (Figure 3.2).

Now, if you are animating a baseball, the scenario is slightly different. Since the baseball is in the air, it doesn't experience the surface friction like the soccer ball, at

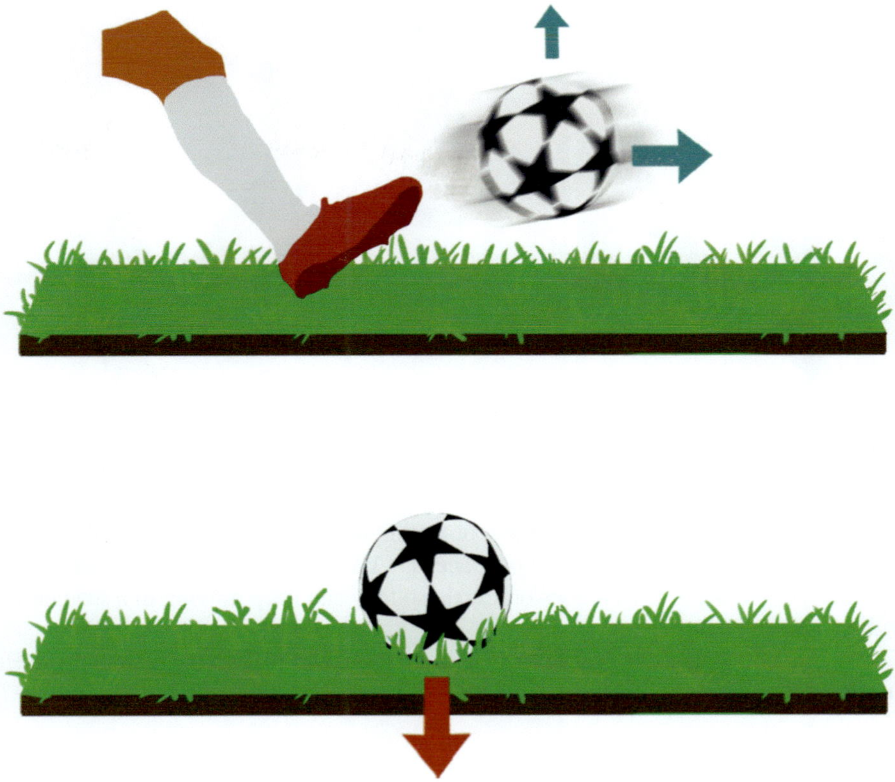

FIGURE 3.2 Image of a soccer ball affected by external forces.

least not until it touches the surface. However, it does encounter air resistance, which creates a drag force, and gravity continues to pull it towards the ground. Over time, the baseball also loses speed and eventually comes to a stop, just like any other object on the planet.

Remember that the same concepts of forward force, gravity, and air resistance are applied when animating a character or creature. When jumping, the trajectory is unlikely to change; the difference lies in the push, as the energy comes from a limb rather than an external force. At this moment, the upward and forward forces are at their peak; therefore, a character's jump initiates much faster than when it is in mid-air, tracing the arc, also known as hang time. At this point, air resistance, gravity, and the character's mass will overcome the forward momentum, causing the body to follow an arc-shaped trajectory towards the surface. To conclude the landing, the body also accelerates during the fall, since the gravity pull is much stronger than the forward motion.

Imagine your character's hip as you would with a bounce ball; the results will surprise you. After nailing the time and pose, you can add extra flavours, such as squash and stretch, overlap, and offset (Figure 3.3).

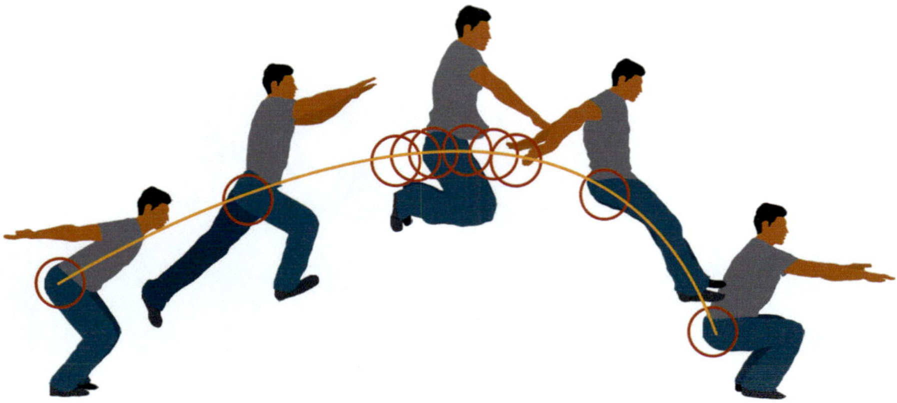

FIGURE 3.3 Image of a character jumping and its similarities to a bounce ball.

So, when do objects actually move in a straight line at a constant speed? You are correct if you answered the vacuum of space, as I know you did. In space, there's no air resistance or atmosphere as it does on Earth, so they can keep moving in a straight line without slowing down.

This is why objects in space, once set in motion, don't stop unless something else interferes.

CHAPTER SUMMARY

- Friction and gravity interfere with an object's ability to remain in a state of motion.
- Objects at rest don't need to be animated, unless an external force acts upon them.
- Inertia is not limited to the state of rest; it also means an object's resistance to any change in its state of motion.
- For the animator, understanding the first law of motion means understanding the subject's composition and the world around them.
- Objects tend to oscillate just before reaching complete rest because of their resistance to changes in motion.
- If you have the chance to animate the environment your character interacts with, you should definitely do so to take the animation to the next level.
- Treating the character as a bouncing ball for some actions, like a jump and landing, can help to understand trajectory and timing.
- In a vacuum, objects tend to move in a straight line at a constant speed unless an external force, such as the object's propulsion, gravitational fields, or gases in space, causes a change to their trajectory.

NOTES

1 Isaac Newton, *Philosophiæ Naturalis Principia Mathematica* (1687).
2 Friction can still exist in space, if objects get in contact with gases and particles.

Newton's Second Law of Motion

4

$F = ma$

Picture two objects with equal mass and acceleration on a collision trajectory towards each other. When this happens, take a moment to consider what happens when the collision occurs.

One thing is certain: Both objects will inflict the same force on each other upon impact. Everything else will depend on several factors we are about to explore.

The first question I would ask is: What is the object's mass and composition? This question is fundamental to your animation: Specifically, how objects will react at the moment of collision. They could rebound off each other, be destroyed, or even merge into one another. Everything depends on the factors previously mentioned. The next question is: What is the acceleration at which they move?

Once you know the objects' composition, you must understand their acceleration to determine how this will affect them.

Since we know the objects are travelling equally at the same speed, the only question is how fast?

During your career, you may face situations where you are required to know the distance per second. This is very common in gameplay animation, where metrics constrain animators. In this chapter, I will show a simple equation for calculating it. However, relying solely on equations for your animation won't achieve the impact that exaggeration and feeling can bring. As an animator, your goal is to use real-life references and add that extra flair to make the animation engaging. In addition, although the calculations are helpful and can help make the animation grounded and believable, they won't prevent you from receiving subjective feedback on your animations. Animation as an art form is subjective. What I might consider fast-moving might not be the same for someone else.

In this chapter, we will explore Newton's second law of motion and gain a deeper understanding of how Force = Mass × Acceleration is a crucial concept in animation. If you are not a math person, don't panic! I will use some examples with formulas, and I encourage you to do this while animating some simple objects to get the hang of it.

DOI: 10.1201/9781003642824-4

Newton's second law is so important because it helps explain why an object with mass doesn't just start moving on its own. You must apply a force greater than the object's resistance to initiate movement and acceleration. In simple terms, this law states that an object's acceleration depends on two factors: the force acting on it and its mass.

To put it even more clearly, acceleration is directly proportional to the force you apply and inversely proportional to the object's mass. The more force you use, the faster it accelerates. But if the object is heavier, you'll need more force to move it the same way.

The second law of motion applies to all forces and explains how any accelerating object moves throughout the universe.

There are formulas to find the object's mass or the force applied to it using Newtons (N),[1] which is the international unit of force measurement and equals 1 kg m/sec^2. Although this is an interesting and useful concept outside the animation environment, I will refrain from showing it here, since there is no real application in animation.

Remember that when it comes to animation, we all know it's not always about strict science. It's about feeling, exaggeration, and readability, and this is up to you to decide how the story is told. However, if you're looking to bring more precision to your work or even feel stuck, here's a useful and practical example to guide you.

During one of the projects I worked on, I needed to find the exact distance a character would move in space to give its run a unique feel. I used a formula to determine the distance this character would move per second. The key here is that this formula works as long as you have the distance provided by the designers or directors, the length of the animation in frames, and the frame rate.

This formula is adaptable to any animation software, frame rate, and metric system. Make sure you adjust the values accordingly.

For example, let's say you want to move a character or object a distance of 5 m over 60 frames, with a frame rate of 30 frames/sec. How do you calculate how many meters per second the character or object will move?

- Distance (m)/Frame length = Result × Frame rate
- 5 m/60 = 0.083
- 0.083 × 30 = 2.5 m/sec

The character will move at a distance of 2.5 m/sec.

Now, if I use the same formula but change the frame rate to 24,

- 5 m/60 = 0.083
- 0.083 × 24 = 2 m/sec.

Keep in mind that if you're not using linear curves, the software will show a different result in the middle of the animation, whereas for linear curves, the middle is always the 1/2 of the final result. Regardless, the final result will always be the same, independent of how your curves look.

Another helpful formula helps you find the time in seconds when you know the frame length and frame rate. It's pretty straightforward if you're working with round numbers for the frame rate, but it can get tricky if you don't.

For example, if you have a frame length of 240 frames and a frame rate of 24 frames/sec, how many seconds will your animation have?

- Frame length/Frame rate = x seconds
- 240/24 = 10 seconds

As I mentioned, the previous one is easy to figure out, but let me make things more interesting. What about an animation with a frame length of 1383 frames at 24 fps?

- 1383/24 = 57.62 seconds animation

It doesn't matter your frame rate or length—you can always find the answer using this simple formula.

4.1 FORCE

It's natural to think of force when it comes to movement—after all, things don't just move for no reason. In animation, it's vital to show exaggeration, solid poses, balance, timing, and silhouette to achieve natural movement.

When a character applies the same force to two objects of different masses, the lighter object will accelerate more than the heavier one. The heavier object might not move at all or might move very slowly.

Understanding the second law of motion will give you an advantage; however, how can you apply this to your animation?

You know that an object has a greater mass than a character trying to push it; you know that to move the object, the character has to apply a greater force on it. Since animation is visual, the poses need to convey a sense of power; light objects don't require the entire character's body to be engaged; you can move a pen with a finger. However, a fridge will need the entire body to be engaged, starting from the pose. A wider stance will help to sell the push and struggle. You need to ensure the feet don't slide, and that the first frames start slowly to convey the sense of weight, taking the object out of its state of rest.

The character's actions should sell this to the audience. Even stylized animation should have a layer of realism so the audience can still follow the story without being distracted (Figure 4.1).

FIGURE 4.1 Image of a character pushing a lighter and heavier object.

4.2 ACCELERATION

The acceleration of an object depends on two variables: the force, as we discussed above, and its mass. In simple terms, an object will accelerate based on the force acting inversely upon its mass.

As an animator, you should consider how quickly your characters and objects will accelerate, depending on their mass and the force acting on them. For example, an elephant will be much slower than a cat because moving its larger mass takes much more force.

Acceleration doesn't necessarily mean distance travelled; don't get confused by that. The same cat can move faster than an elephant; however, a much larger creature, the fantasy type we see in movies, will travel a greater distance compared to the cat. Even if the cat moves faster, the larger creature can cover more distance due to its size.

Studying reference and anatomy is crucial for identifying and addressing these challenges, helping your animation feel more natural and interesting.

4.3 MASS

Mass measures the amount of matter an object contains and is determined by the type and number of atoms in it. For example, 100 kg of cotton and 100 kg of iron have the same mass but different volumes due to their different densities.

If I asked you what is heavier, 100 kg of iron or 100 kg of cotton, what would you say?

I imagine you answer that both have exactly the same weight; however, which one has the greater volume? What would you say?

Cotton will definitely have a greater volume per 100 kg because it has more space between its atoms than iron does, in addition to its material composition, which makes

FIGURE 4.2 Image of a scale comparing iron and cotton.

it much lighter when compared in volume with iron. On the other hand, due to the space between its cellulose fibres, cotton can be compressed much more easily than iron.

In animation and real life, the result is the same if you apply the same force and acceleration to 100 kg of cotton or iron. However, to make the animation realistic, you'd need to show that the cotton volume is much larger than the iron (Figure 4.2).

CHAPTER SUMMARY

- Before starting an animation, it is important to consider the object's mass, acceleration, force applied onto or from it, and composition.
- Formulas and math are very useful; however, consider the exaggeration factor if necessary to support the story.
- Precision is very important when dealing with metrics in gameplay animation.
- The same force applied to objects of distinct masses will result in different accelerations.
- Acceleration refers to how an object's speed changes over time, not the distance it covers.
- Mass indicates the quantity of matter in an object, which depends on the type and number of atoms present.
- Volume doesn't refer to how heavy the object is, but rather its composition.

NOTE

1 A newton (N) is the international unit of measure for force. One newton equals to 1 kilogram meter per second squared: $1\ N = 1\ kg\ m/s^2$.

Newton's Third Law *Action and Reaction*

5

You've probably heard the saying, "For every action, there's a reaction," but have you ever thought about what that means in physics and animation?

Picture the following scenario. A person wakes up, gets out of bed, walks to the bathroom to brush their teeth and shower, then walks to the kitchen to get a cup of coffee, and finally sits on the couch to enjoy this nice hot beverage.

These actions, part of our daily routine that we don't give much thought to, involve applying the third law of motion an uncountable number of times, which can be hard to comprehend.

The action of pushing off the bed to get up is equal to the force of the bed against the person. And yes, the third law also applies to objects at rest, like a bed. The only difference is that the mattress, bed frame, and surface combined have much more resistance than a human body.

When this person gets up and slightly shifts their weight for balance, more force is applied against the mattress at the pressure point, causing the bed and mattress to react and prevent buckling under the subject's weight. You know, getting out of bed can sometimes require a lot of force, at least for me.

The moment this person stands up, the floor pushes them up as the subject pushes the floor down. For every step taken, the person is pushing the floor as the floor pushes in the opposite direction.

Actions like grabbing the toothbrush and applying toothpaste to it, water contacting the person's body, grabbing a towel and drying the body, walking to the kitchen, grabbing a cup of coffee, and sitting on a couch, there was always a force playing against it, making the third law of motion happen several times.

Newton's third law of motion states that for every action, there's an equal and opposite reaction. I always emphasize "equal and opposite" when explaining the third law in classes because it is crucial to happen since every movement in nature requires an opposing force to make it happen. In fact, the third law of motion also applies to objects at rest. For example, when a subject is standing, sitting, or at rest on a surface, the force exerted on the surface is equal and opposite to the force on the subject, creating a perfect balance.

DOI: 10.1201/9781003642824-5

As we wrap up our introduction to Newton's laws, I want to highlight why the third law is my favourite. It ties together everything from the first two laws and shows how much ahead of his time Newton's thoughts were. You can't talk about animation without considering it.

In fact, everything in animation depends on the third law to set things in motion, and animation can't exist without this. In my opinion, the topic is the most important, as it consolidates all the other topics in this book.

When a person walks, their feet push against the ground backwards and downwards, and the surface responds with an opposite reaction, pushing forward and upwards. Since a human's mass is very small compared to the ground's mass, the reaction is proportional to the person's mass, and the only thing that moves is the person pushing against the surface.

A gun, when fired, must recoil because of the powerful force of the projectile moving forward. The gunpowder and gas produced when pulling the trigger ignite the projectile in the chamber, and the only escape route is from the muzzle. This energy is not lost; it recoils in the opposite direction.

Imagine dropping a ball on the ground. Gravity pull it downwards, accelerating until it hits the surface. The combined downward force of the ball's mass and gravity causes it to crash into a much larger mass when it contacts the ground. The acceleration increases before contact; depending on the altitude, the object can reach terminal velocity. Therefore, keep in mind that the acceleration on any body in free fall is constantly increasing as it falls. That said, in this example, the speed increases as the object falls until it comes to a stop. When the contact occurs, the acceleration changes from X speed to zero, and guess what? The ball bounces back up.

Gravity constantly pulls the ball down, so it doesn't bounce back as high as it was dropped. For every bounce, the ball loses energy. As gravity pulls the object towards the surface, its acceleration decreases until it reaches a state of rest.

But the ball's material and the energy from the ground at the moment of contact are key. When the ball hits the ground, the ground pushes back with equal and opposite force, causing the ball to bounce back up. This is a perfect example of Newton's third law in action: For every force, there's an equal and opposite reaction (Figure 5.1).

Picture someone pushing a heavy box. They're using their whole body, leaning in with all their strength. As their legs push against the ground, friction helps keep them steady, allowing them to apply force in the opposite direction. At the same time, the ground pushes back on their legs, giving them more power to move forward. Meanwhile, the box is fighting back, resisting the push.

At this moment, the box can either remain in place, offering sufficient resistance to prevent movement, or the person can push with enough force to move it. In the end, it's a contest between these two forces. However, in the example above, if the box offers less resistance, less force will be required from all aspects.

There are a few ways the concepts of weight, timing, and poses relate to the third law of motion. Can you think of any?

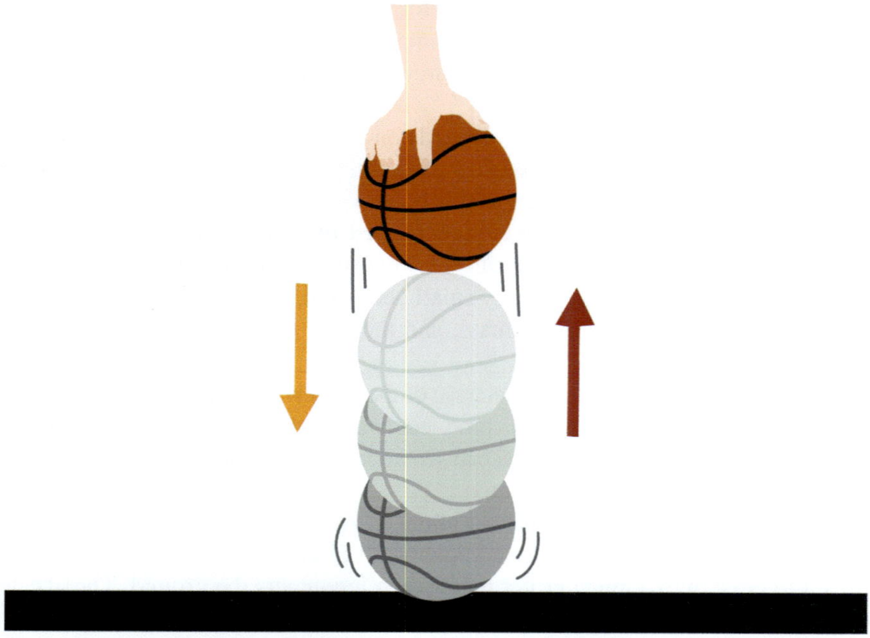

FIGURE 5.1 Image of a ball bouncing and its reaction force.

5.1 WEIGHT

When a character tries to move an object, there is a fight between the character and the object's reaction force. As the character exceeds the force needed to overcome the object's weight, it will start to move. If less force is applied, the object won't budge. With that in mind, the animation must use poses and timing to convey the object's weight, creating a sense of naturalness.

Another example to explore the sense of weight could be a character itself. Understanding weight is important when considering pressure points: For every action we take during a walk, run, or even a weight shift, we apply a concentrated force to objects, creating a pressure at the contact point. With that in mind, any character that comes into contact with a surface, objects, or other characters will exert these pressures against the other. Now, if the other object or character is smaller in mass, the first character will apply force where the contact occurs. For example, imagine a heavier character trying to land on a much lighter surface; at the point of contact, the surface will bend or break.

However, if we change the scenario and have the character land on a much heavier surface, like concrete, the result is the transfer of energy from the character to the surface and back from the surface to the character, causing the character to squat due to the sheer force. Every scenario has its consequences, so make sure to understand your character's surroundings.

5.2 TIMING

Picture a character walking. As we discussed earlier in this chapter, there is a continuous effort to push against the ground to generate enough force for movement. For example, a slow walk feels relaxed and less engaged. However, friction and pushing are still present, as they are essential for movement, but they are less intense than during a fast stride. A faster walk engages more of the body, and it feels firmer. The push is more purposeful and stronger, helping to speed up the walk. In other words, more force pushing against the ground results in quicker movements.

In another scenario, consider a character jumping. A short jump requires less push against the ground and consequently less energy from the body. The character doesn't need to crouch down very low to gather energy, just enough to cover the desired distance. As a result, the energy transfer from the ground back to the character is smaller, making the jump shorter and faster. In comparison, a longer jump demands more push and energy from the character, so the force against the surface is greater, resulting in a longer distance and more hanging time until landing.

5.3 POSE

Posing the character is the final fundamental of animation correlated to the third law of motion. Balanced characters, well-defined silhouettes, and proper weight distribution are not only ways to make the animation appealing and readable, but also a basis for the motion about to happen.

Imagine a scenario where a character needs to move a very heavy object. The stance and contact points are important to make the action believable; otherwise, the audience won't engage with the animation and story. In this scenario, the animator should widen the character's legs for balance and engage the upper body as it pushes the object, or perhaps use their back to contact the object as the legs push it. There are several ways to approach this, and the animator can use their imagination to explore different poses. However, it is impossible to move a heavy object without proper mechanics (Figure 5.2).

The fundamental knowledge is that your animation needs to translate that struggle and show the audience what's at play.

But here's the most important thing: There is always a reaction in the opposite direction, no matter who's winning. Understanding this balance of forces is crucial for creating realistic movement and action (Figure 5.3).

It is important to note that the reaction that causes objects to move, although it always occurs, also depends on the surface or fluid's composition. An object stranded in space, such as an astronaut for this example, can move but will not go anywhere without a system to propel them or without falling into a gravitational field. In space, where vacuum is predominant, there is nothing to push against to go anywhere.

FIGURE 5.2 Image of a person pushing a small box with their finger.

FIGURE 5.3 Image of a person pushing a heavy box.

A swimmer, for example, pushes against the water to start and maintain motion. Due to its composition, this movement can be slower than walking; however, water provides some resistance for the push, even if less than the ground, but much more than air, for instance.

To consolidate the knowledge, imagine a soccer game in which a player lines up to take a shot at the goal, while the goalkeeper is ready to block it. Now, let's break down how Newton's third law of motion plays out step by step.

The player's support leg pushes against the ground, utilizing friction to maintain balance and generate sufficient power for the shot. The kicking leg then strikes the ball, propelling it forward. But here's the catch: As the player's foot pushes the ball, the ball pushes back with an equal and opposite force. Since the ball has much less mass than the player, it flies towards the goal, but the player's body also reacts to the ball's force, even if it is smaller. Now, when the goalkeeper grabs the ball, they push against the ground with both legs to maintain balance, and the ground pushes back, helping the goalkeeper stay stable. Still full of energy from the kick, the ball crashes into the goalkeeper's hands. The ball's acceleration changes from X to very close to zero until the contact is fully absorbed by the goalkeeper, and the ball comes to rest (Figure 5.4).

FIGURE 5.4 Image of a soccer player kicking a ball while a goalkeeper catches it.

The idea that we're pushing in the opposite direction of the ground while the ground pushes us back can feel a bit counterintuitive. You might wonder, "How can we push the ground?" Well, think about the planet's mass compared to everything else here. Earth's mass is about six trillion trillion kilograms, and its gravitational field is strong enough to have its moon and occasionally pull some asteroids into our atmosphere. Now, with that information, when you push against the ground, giving you enough energy to walk, run, or play ball, you know that your relatively tiny mass will always be influenced by the far greater mass of the planet.

CHAPTER SUMMARY

- The third law of motion applies to both objects in motion and at rest.
- The forces applied to both objects are equal and opposite.
- A reaction force that causes objects to rebound is the result of the equal and opposite force applied where the object contacts, like a surface, along with its composition.
- Animators should analyse and use references to understand how the objects will react with each other before starting to animate the scene.
- Your animation should sell the idea of weight through strong poses and timing.
- In a vacuum, there is nothing to generate push, and the third law only applies if the object enters a gravitational field, contacts something like debris or satellites, or has its own way to propel.
- Consider the composition of what the character is in contact with.
- Remember that the force applied to an object may not have any reaction whatsoever, depending on its composition and mass.

Balance 6

To start this chapter, let us try an experiment. If possible, stand as straight as you can with your feet centred and close together. Now, relax your arms. I am sure you can hold this pose for a while. Now, what happens next if you take one foot off the ground, with no movement of your hips or arms? You lose your balance, and if you don't do a weight shift or put your foot back on the ground, you will eventually fall.

If you raise one foot and bring it as close as possible to your centre of mass, you will most likely be able to keep your balance since your body is aligned with your supporting leg. The wider you spread your leg, the further your centre of mass is from your contact point, dramatically unbalancing you when on one legs (Figure 6.1).

It would be possible to counter the centre of mass if you could stretch your arm from the same side as the contact leg and hold a weight heavy enough to support the lack of balance from the raised leg. Although this scenario is unlikely due to the sheer strength required of your muscles and joints, and depending on how wide the foot is, it may not be visually appealing in animation; however, it is technically a solution to maintaining balance (Figure 6.2).

How do you think an imbalance happens if the subject's mass remains unchanged? By getting on one foot, a person's weight doesn't simply change; it remains the same, but the same would still fall. This is due to the mass, contact points, and weight distribution.

In the example above, when someone stands on one foot, the volume of the upper body remains constant. The change in the contact point supporting the mass leads to poor balance and eventually to collapse.

For better understanding, when discussing mass, distribution, and contact points, for example, I like to think of the strongest geometric shape: the triangle.

Starting with the mass, the top is narrower than the base, making it naturally lighter since it carries less volume. In this design, the weight is evenly distributed to the base. The compression from the top volume encounters resistance from the much larger contact points and mass, which are evenly distributed across all sides. This resistance eases the compression of the top due to its volume and the distribution of contact points. The result is a highly balanced object. Now, shifting to a 3D environment, what geometric shape can you think of that is similar to a triangle? If you answered a pyramid, you're correct.

Next time you animate, think about the triangle and its three pillars of balance: mass, contact point, and how the weight is distributed. For any animation, this is a solid basis for building balanced characters.

DOI: 10.1201/9781003642824-6

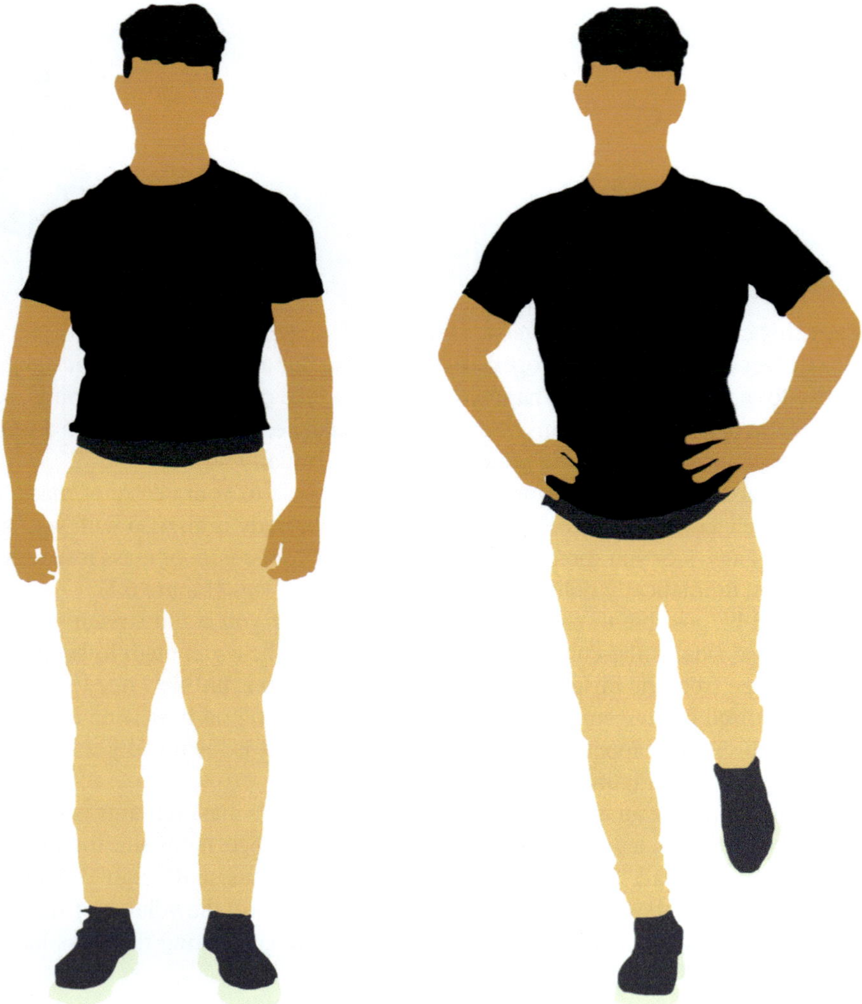

FIGURE 6.1 Image of two people balancing with two and one leg.

Consider any martial arts and their stances using the triangle as a reference. You will likely see a wider, balanced stance, with the weight distributed across the legs in a triangular pattern. A wide stance has many uses in a fight: balance, as we just learned, keeps the fighter stable and harder to take down when a pull, push, or strike occurs.

The other reason for a wider stance is mobility; in a combat situation, the fighter must be able to move faster, either for reach or dodge. Widening the stance too much with straight legs should provide some balance and limit movements if a faster reaction is needed. This is due to the lack of bending at the knees, which results in a loss of thrust. On the other hand, adopting a narrow stance with straight legs will not only lack balance but also reduce mobility.

FIGURE 6.2 Image of a person balancing on one leg with a weight.

The sweet spot is on the stances fighters use, and there is a science to it. They provide enough space between the fighter's legs for an optimal balance and a slight bending of the knees that can be used for faster reactions. In these situations, they can use their legs as a spring to propel themselves quickly towards the target.

It doesn't matter if you're working on an action or a more subtle animation; balance supports stronger silhouettes, making your work grounded and appealing.

Observing the diagram below, it is possible to visualize how the load, pressure point, and compression from weight distribution work. For simple shapes like the triangle, it's easier to understand; however, when discussing characters, remember to observe their mass, shape, contact points, and direction. Once in motion, the trajectory can help identify the character's weight distribution for a better balance (Figure 6.3).

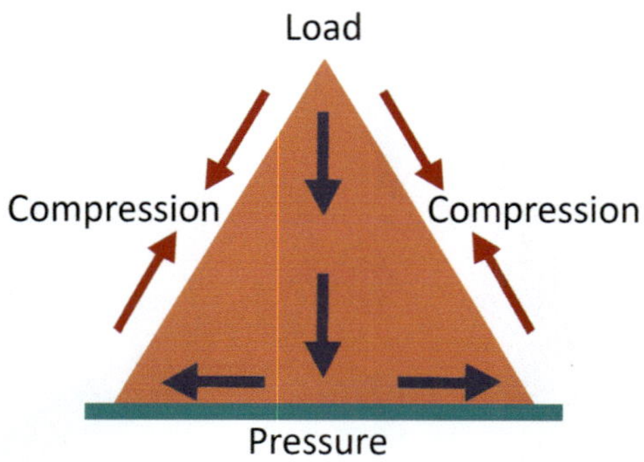

FIGURE 6.3 Image of a triangle representing load, compression, and pressure.

A good observation exercise I like to use to test my students' comprehension regarding balance is the one with two people walking downhill. In both images from Figure 6.4, the students can easily see that people are walking down a slope due to the tilt and silhouette of their bodies. Of course, the environment also plays a role, aiding in the understanding of decline. The key difference is that in the image on the left, the person rotates their feet to create friction with the surface, keeping their body straight for the viewer's frame of reference. This makes the slope walk appear more like walking on a flat surface and feel much more natural. In contrast, the figure on the right shows the other person leaning awkwardly forward, which clearly indicates a lack of balance. However, not everyone notices this right away; they see that something seems off, but figuring out what can be challenging.

When comparing both images, it all comes down to the centre of mass. The centre of mass is right where the foot contacts the surface, supporting the person's weight, and it remains there for every step, following the hip, similar to a regular walk.

On the other hand, the illustration on the right in Figure 6.4, lacks proper balance because the centre of mass isn't positioned under the person's foot and hip. Since this isn't happening, the first issue is the absence of friction from the supporting foot, followed by the distance from the foot to the subject's centre of mass, which is ahead of the foot around the core and torso, which, as you know, should be under the foot. When this isn't the case, it results in loss of balance, a fall, and perhaps a few broken bones (Figure 6.4).

In animation, balance is an essential aspect of Solid Drawing, one of the 12 principles of animation. You may also hear about balance in how characters are framed on screen or even in terms of colour, but don't worry, that's not what we're focusing on here. A simple way to balance a character is to pose it asymmetrically; failing to do so often results in weak and unappealing poses, ultimately leading to poor animation. Posing the character asymmetrically makes its silhouette much more interesting and enhances its negative space.

Here's an example of two characters in a standing, idle pose, which is very common in video game scenarios. In both figures, the characters are balanced; however, note how one feels more natural while the other feels flat and rigid. Keep in mind that both poses can work, but they will deliver different results (Figure 6.5).

FIGURE 6.4 Image of two people walking downhill: unbalanced vs. balanced.

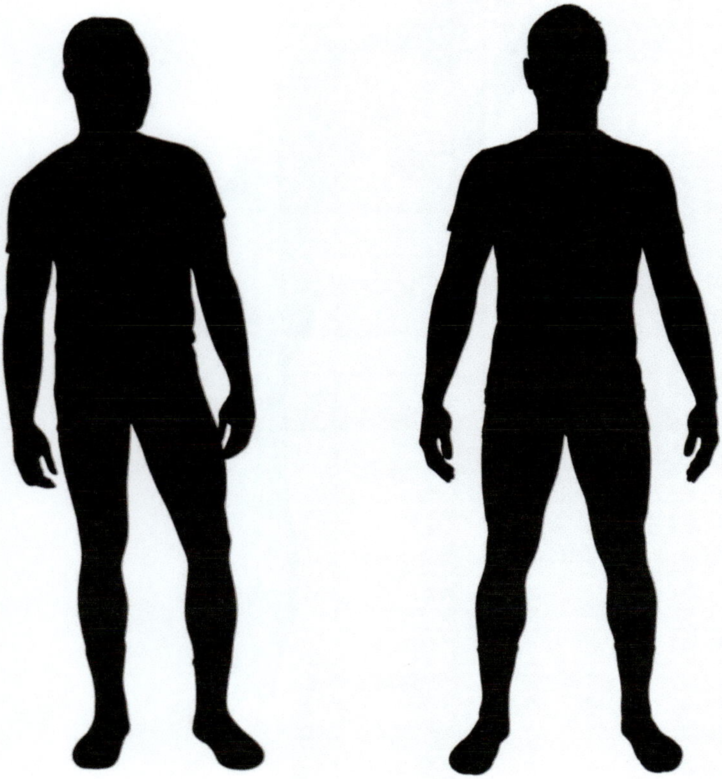

FIGURE 6.5 Image of two silhouettes in an idle pose.

There is nothing wrong with either character. The animator is telling the story through poses and movement, and the delivery should align with this goal.

Although many video game players often disregard the idle pose, this is the animation the character returns to when the controller or keyboard is not in use. The idle pose gives the character identity and can transition to a combat stance, walk, crouch, jump, etc. The animation and the animator are key parts of the story, conveying essential gameplay and story elements, as well as the message the character should deliver through its performance and identity, aligned with the story's vision.

For more subtle animations, where the movement is slow, spotting an unbalanced character is much easier. As the figure shows, an unbalanced character stretching feels unappealing and less dynamic. However, the problem is the reaction that precedes an unbalanced pose. When this pose is not intentional, what follows is anything but a character tipping over backwards, trying to find its balance. At this moment, the animator made a fundamental error, since the natural reaction would be, in fact, the character losing the balance (Figure 6.6).

FIGURE 6.6 Image of a person stretching unbalanced.

On the other hand, in faster animations, the eyes can be driven to follow the flow and continuity, and often this results in unbalanced elements being disregarded. This is due to the fast reaction that precedes the previous pose, as long as the trajectory feels right.

A simple run cycle, with only a few key poses, can exhibit moments where the character appears unbalanced, which is entirely natural. Don't expect to achieve balanced poses at all times when reviewing your animation frame by frame. Instead, consider the continuity and mechanics of the movement. Ask questions like what forces are driving the character and what poses are natural for maintaining continuity in the animation. However, when assessing the character's movement for every frame, respect the spacing and other principles for a cleaner and more natural result (Figure 6.7).

FIGURE 6.7 Image of a person running in "Up" pose.

To truly understand balance in animation, it's crucial to grasp the concepts of gravity and the three laws of motion—concepts with which you're hopefully more familiar now.

Earlier in this book, I mentioned how we constantly battle gravity, which continuously acts on us. We refer to this as the reaction force. When animating, it's easy to overlook the impact of gravity on your character because the paper or software you're using doesn't remind you of it.

A simple way to understand balance and reaction force is as follows: If all the forces acting on an object are balanced, two things happen: either the object remains at rest, due to inertia, or moves at a constant speed, such as when it reaches terminal velocity. For example, imagine a falling object; as you might know, gravity is one of the forces acting upon it. On the other side, there's a force pushing against the object that eventually equals the object's mass and the gravity acting on it. Air resistance, as discussed in Chapter 2, and friction, a little further in the book, are reaction forces. When both forces are balanced, terminal velocity occurs. In other words, balance can happen either at rest or in motion.

If balance acts on objects at rest or in motion, you can easily assume that Newton's laws of motion overlap with this idea, and you are right! In both physics and animation, things don't just happen on their own; some opposing force must exist for equilibrium to occur. The only example where the laws of physics do not apply—and I can confidently say this also holds in animation, as of the time I am writing this book—is in the singularity of a black hole, where all its matter is condensed at its centre. Gravity is immensely strong, such that spacetime and the laws of physics simply cease to exist. On the other hand, some believe that things exist inside a black hole, and our entire universe is in one right now.

Remember that throughout your career, your characters will have different masses and shapes, so balance will always be something to consider, but it won't always look the same for every character.

During your journey, characters will have different shapes, sizes, physiologies, and even personalities, which affect how they move. As an animator, studying anatomy and reference is crucial to achieving a believable product. Understanding the character's story and motivation is as essential as the laws of motion and physics, and finding the balance to achieve the best results for your product is crucial.

An example of balance at work in popular culture that most people will be familiar with is the use of anti-gravity shoes, worn by singer Michael Jackson and his dancers for performances of Smooth Criminal. The device allowed them to lean forward at an angle of 45°, defying gravity by shifting their centre of mass, where any person would simply fall due to the lack of balance.

Watching that dance move was impressive, and I have to admit, as a child, I really believed it was possible. As impressive as the feat was, it couldn't be performed without the shoes and the stage mechanism onto which the shoes' heels are locked to perform the dance move safely.

As you can see, shifting the centre of mass redistributes the weight and pressure to other areas. Without proper balance, anything will collapse.

6.1 CENTRE OF MASS

The centre of mass of an object is the point where the entire weight can be considered to act. It's easy to find the centre of mass for symmetrical objects—look where the lines of symmetry cross. For instance, the centre of mass of a cube will be exactly at its geometric centre (Figure 6.8).

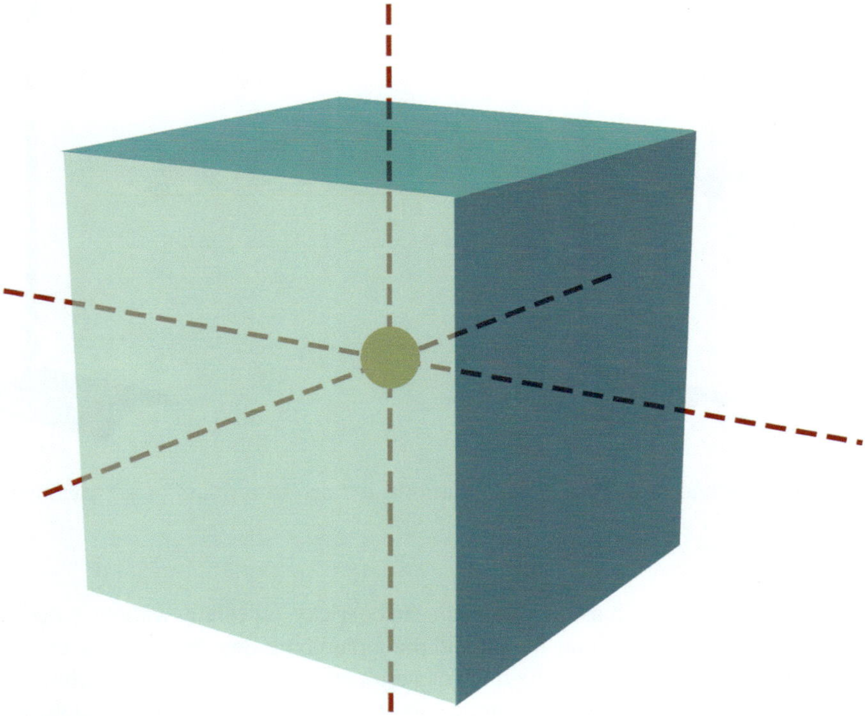

FIGURE 6.8 Image of a cube showing the centre of mass and the geometric centre.

Finding the centre of mass gets trickier when the object isn't perfectly symmetrical, but you can try a few real-life methods. One is the hanging method, which attaches a plumb bob to this irregular object at two points. The object must be freely pivoting from the stand to let gravity and its shape settle naturally.

After that, the string will form a straight line due to gravity, connecting the two points. Where the lines intersect, that's the centre of mass. Another method involves placing the object on a table and slowly moving it towards the edge until it falls off. Rotate the object 90° and repeat. The point where the lines cross is the centre of mass. Please don't try this with any expensive objects; in fact, I wouldn't recommend it at all (Figure 6.9).

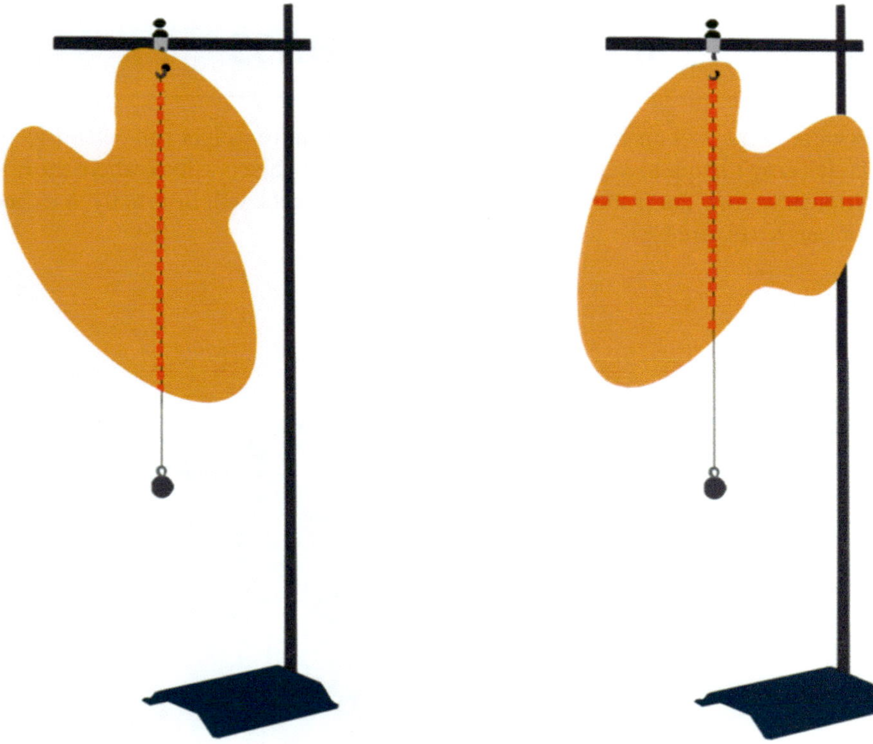

FIGURE 6.9 Image of a plumb bob measuring the centre of mass of an asymmetrical object.

Finding the centre of mass in animation can be tricky, especially without experience. It's all about visuals; you cannot weigh and pin a plumbing line on the character, and it must be appealing when seen through the camera's eyes. Before starting to animate, it is vital to study the character and use your eyes to find its centre of mass and what its weight distribution will be when posing it. Remember that the centre of mass will change continuously as you animate. If you are working on a movie or game cinematic, you could potentially get away with some characters feeling unbalanced since everything behind the camera will never be seen, and as long as it feels right through the camera's eyes, people will never notice. However, gameplay and VR content may not be so simple since you usually have freedom over the camera control. On the other hand, gameplay animation is all about feeling and responsiveness. Hence, if you must push a character-defying balance for a few frames to achieve a responsive and more engaging experience, go for it!

A good way to find the centre of mass of a character is to draw a line where you think it should be. If the mass feels evenly distributed on both sides, you've got it right! If not, adjust the line left or right and see how it feels. When tracing the lines, remember to consider the mass for each limb and pressure points. If the character is carrying a prop, like an enormous axe or a shield, or prosthetics, like a giant arm, etc. This will influence how the centre of mass is distributed and eventually how the character will be animated.

Always consider your character's mass and pose. Every character and every pose will have its distinct centre of mass based on how they are designed (Figure 6.10).

FIGURE 6.10 Image of balanced and unbalanced characters.

CHAPTER SUMMARY

- When thinking about balance, it is important to consider the subject's mass, contact point, and weight distribution.
- Remember that the surface the character stands on will affect how they are balanced, and the poses should be polished to support the centre of mass.

- The character's pose can feel stiff and mirrored, if the story is asking for it; however, in most cases, this is not applicable.
- When working on more subtle animations, the lack of balance can be more easily spotted.
- Balance can occur either at rest or while in motion.
- Sometimes unbalanced animations can be ignored if they support a strong performance, or if the way the character is framed doesn't reveal it.

Projectile Motion 7

Imagine someone jumping forward, like an athlete competing for the gold medal in the long jump at the Olympic Games. Once the athlete is in motion towards the sandpit, can their trajectory be changed?

The answer is no; it would be physically impossible for the athlete to rely solely on their body to change their trajectory. Once the athlete's body is in motion and in the air, gravity and air resistance are the only forces acting on it. The athlete's push upward and forward is powerful, as they propel themselves into the air with their body as the initial thrust. At this moment, the forward motion is stronger than air resistance and gravity, but that quickly changes; hence, we don't see people jumping too high or far relying only on their bodies. Conversely, jumping on a planet or body with much lower gravity and escape velocity could significantly increase this jump or even launch the person into space. However, on Earth, gravity always wins, and it won't be long before the athlete's push loses energy. This occurs due to vertical and horizontal motion, which are forces acting on objects in the air. Let me break this down using the long jump example above. When the initial jump happens, there's a significant force from the athlete's momentum gained from a run. According to the first law of motion, an object in motion tends to stay in motion, which creates considerable distance from the point where the athlete crouches, combined with the acceleration from the run, enabling a long-distance jump. In animation, this concept is known as timing and spacing.

The vertical motion is the force acting on projectiles when they are launched in an upward trajectory, as in the jump example above, until gravity pulls the athlete downwards—in other words, the up-and-down motion. Horizontal motion, on the other hand, is the force that moves projectiles forward, backwards, left, or right. As gravity influences vertical motion, air resistance affects horizontal motion. The reason why a projectile creates an arc-shaped trajectory is due to the initial force from the launch and the influence of gravity and air resistance on the object (Figure 7.1).

In a different scenario, imagine someone throwing a balloon in the air. What will the trajectory be like? Well, this is much trickier and more unpredictable because the balloon's mass is much smaller than a human's, and it's filled with air. However, the balloon will fall because, although the rubber material is light, it is still heavier than air.

If the balloon is filled with helium gas instead of air, you know what will happen: The balloon will rise because helium is lighter than air and strong enough to carry the rubber material along with it.

A fun fact about balloons is that their trajectory is difficult to predict because we can't see the air surrounding the balloon. Since the balloon is filled with air and made

DOI: 10.1201/9781003642824-7

FIGURE 7.1 Image of a long jump athlete leaping into the sandpit, with horizontal and vertical lines.

> Horizontal motion can work independently or in conjunction with vertical motion and is characterized by the speed at which an object travels along a horizontal path.
>
> It is correct to say that horizontal motion can occur at a constant speed if air resistance is disregarded, as gravity is the only force acting on the object.

of light rubber, it can't carry enough mass to follow a precise arc like a heavier object. However, both vertical and horizontal motions will always affect the balloon and any other light object, as long as they have mass.

In physics and some animation software, horizontal motion is represented by the *X* value: $+x$ to the right and $-x$ to the left, while vertical motion is represented by the *Y* value: $+y$ for upward motion and $-y$ for downward motion. (Figure 7.2).

If you are wondering whether it is possible to avoid gravity's vertical pull to prevent an object from eventually crashing onto the surface, the answer is yes; this is done all the time with satellites. Have you thought about how they can stay in orbit without dropping from the sky? In fact, they are constantly dropping from the sky. To put a satellite into orbit, a rocket is launched carrying it. The rocket overcomes the force of gravity at an incredible speed and leaves the Earth's atmosphere. It deploys the satellites at the desired location. The rocket's momentum accelerates the satellite to speeds over 20.000 km/h. This constant acceleration, combined with the lack of air resistance, allows the satellite to travel without friction. This momentum is so great that even with the pull of gravity towards the planet, the object moves in a state of free fall without crashing into Earth, as long as it is deployed at the correct location and speed.

FIGURE 7.2 Image of horizontal and vertical motion acting on a character.

Have you ever noticed that some projectiles can travel along a curved path once launched? This is easily seen in sports like soccer, baseball, and many others. The force exerted on some objects is called The Magnus effect, where the projectile's spin causes an imbalance in the pressure from the faster and slower spinning sides, creating a curved path.

It is important to note that deformations on the object's surface, like gaps, dimples or stitches, and the speed at which the object spins, will cause more curvature on the path. The smoother the object is, the less the influence of the Magnus effect will be.

In 1997, during the Tournoi de France, Brazilian soccer player Roberto Carlos made history with the well-known "Impossible" free-kick against France. At a distance of 35 m and a speed of 136 km, some people say that Roberto Carlos defied physics with his free-kick, where the ball overshoots the left side of the goal to eventually find its way on a curved trajectory, leaving goalkeeper Fabien Barthez with no reaction. As someone watching this match and finding this free kick impressive, I cannot say that Roberto Carlos defied physics; it was a feat and deserves to be remembered, but the final score of 1–1 resulted from physics and demonstrates the Magnus effect at work (Figure 7.3).

FIGURE 7.3 Image of the impossible free kick ball's trajectory.

Let me show you a few more different scenarios to exemplify what we have been learning in this chapter. Picture two identical balls dropped off a cliff from the same height, one launched horizontally and the other, simply dropped. Which ball will hit the ground first? The answer is that both will hit the ground simultaneously. This might sound counterintuitive since you would imagine that the ball travelling further would remain in the air longer due to the addition of horizontal motion, but in fact, the explanation is simple. Both forces act independently, and horizontal motion is measured by the distance the object travels from its origin, while vertical motion is measured by the height at which the object falls. Since both are falling from the same height, the distance the ball lands doesn't matter, as gravity is the only force pulling it down.

What happens to each ball is: As the thrown ball moves through space, air resistance slows its horizontal motion, while gravity pulls the object downwards, creating a parabola or curved path towards the surface where it will eventually land. In this scenario, both forces act on the ball but operate independently. As the ball travels horizontally, the vertical motion caused by gravity increases until the two forces balance, at which point the object hits the surface.

Meanwhile, the ball that is dropped is not affected by horizontal motion, but just as vertical motion influences the object that was thrown, it will also affect the one that was dropped.

Unlike objects, animated characters can use body mechanics to drive motion. Their limbs propel them in a particular direction, like a jump in a parkour performance, a fight scene, or even a hop to avoid a pothole. Once the direction is set and the character is in the air, they cannot change direction without help from external factors. At this moment, the character behaves as a projectile, and vertical and horizontal motion will act on it as it would on any other object (Figure 7.4).

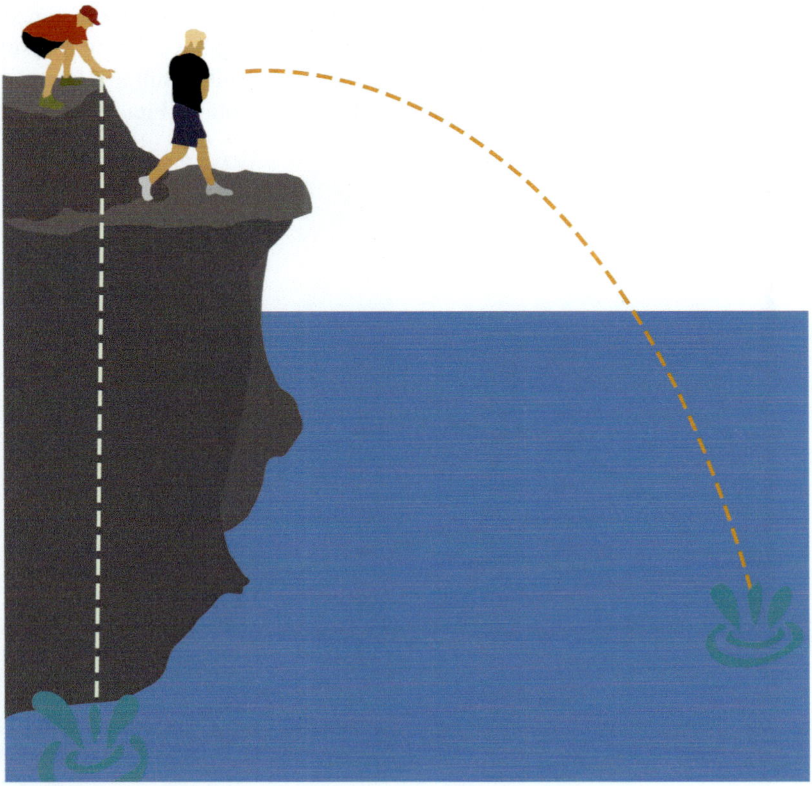

FIGURE 7.4 Image of two objects being thrown and dropped along a trajectory.

For the following example of projectile motion, I like to think of a cannon shooting an iron ball. If the goal is to achieve a further distance for the cannonball to reach the ground, what would be the best way to position the cannon?

At an angle of 90°, straight up, since there's no horizontal motion, the cannonball will return to its origin; however, if the goal is to keep the cannonball in the air for the longest time, shooting at a 90° angle will give the best results. In this scenario, the iron ball will stay in the air longer and land around the same spot, as we discussed with the dropped ball example above. Do you know why this ball stays in the air longer than at other angles? Because in a cannon, the balls aren't being dropped from the same altitude; they are fired at different angles and reach various heights and distances. The iron ball that reaches the highest peak stays in the air for a longer duration.

Suppose you lower the cannon to a 75° angle and shoot the iron ball. The distance reached will be greater than when fired from an angle of 90°, but the altitude will be much lower. The cannonball will not stay airborne for long since it is much closer to the ground, and you know that at the moment the ball leaves the cannon, gravity will start pulling it towards the ground.

However, setting the cannon to a 45° angle would yield the best distance. From this angle, the cannonball is neither too straight to land at the exact location nor too low to be closer to the ground, making it the best angle for a shot with greater distance using vertical and horizontal motion. In other words, any angle above 45° will result in a higher altitude and a shorter distance; any angle below 45° will result in a lower altitude but also a shorter distance due to horizontal and vertical motion (Figure 7.5).

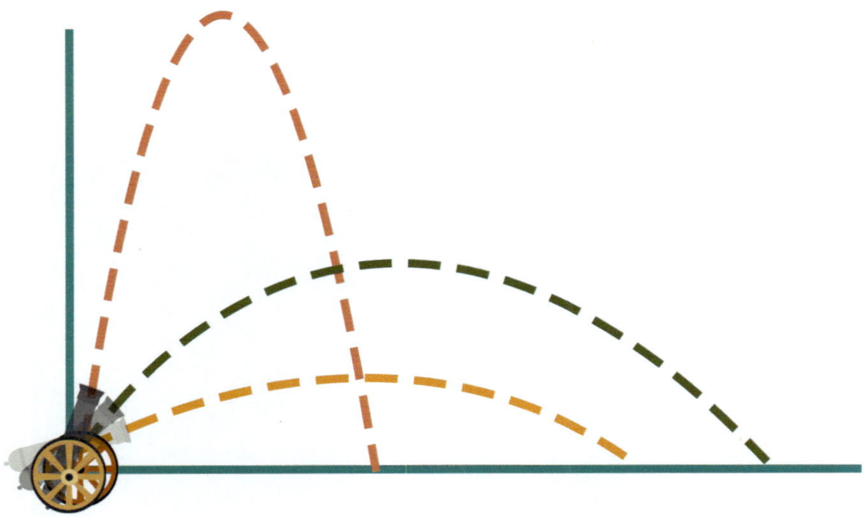

FIGURE 7.5 Image showing a cannonball's trajectory at various angles and results.

7.1 THE CORIOLIS EFFECT

Now that you better understand projectile motion, the next step is to grasp how an object's trajectory can be affected when travelling much larger distances.

The Coriolis effect results from the Earth's rotation and affects the path objects travel, causing them to trace a curved trajectory rather than a straight line. It influences aircraft, air and ocean currents, projectiles, and other atmospheric events, such as hurricanes.

Let me break this down for you. As you may know, the planet spins counterclockwise towards the east. This spin is greater around the line of the Equator due to the larger area to be covered in one full rotation and much smaller in the northern and southern hemispheres. This difference in speed causes objects to turn to the right in the northern hemisphere and to the left in the southern hemisphere.

Even if we don't feel the difference when travelling to either hemisphere or near the equator line, since we are smoothly spinning, at constant speed along with the planet and pinned by the force of gravity.

This force acts independently of the force of gravity, but they work together to influence objects like missiles or bullets.

A long-range shooter needs to consider gravity, air resistance, drag, and the Coriolis effect when aiming at a target. The farther away a target is, the more difficult it becomes to hit. At longer distances, aiming at an angle is necessary to offset the projectile's downward motion due to gravity. Observing the surroundings and studying the wind for changes is crucial to hitting the target. Air resistance, pressure, and the shape of the projectile are other essential factors to consider. Finally, the curvature of the planet and the path the projectile takes result from the Coriolis effect; objects travelling from the southern hemisphere to the equator curve to the left, while objects from the northern hemisphere to the equator curve to the right. All of this needs to be taken into consideration (Figure 7.6).

FIGURE 7.6 Image of the Coriolis effect.

The projectile's shape and the speed at which it travels can determine how the offset from the target should be aimed; the higher the speed and distance from the target, the lesser the curvature due to gravity and the Coriolis effect.

A fun experiment that can be done at home to test the Coriolis effect with two simple objects is to use a pen and a small ball. I tried with a lacrosse ball, but you can use any other spherical object that can be marked with a pen.

Start marking the southern and northern hemispheres. From the south side, trace a straight line as you rotate the ball while the planet spins to your right. You will notice that the line curves to your left. Now, repeating the test, go to the north side and draw the same line from the starting point as you rotate the ball. Remember, this time the ball must rotate towards your left side. The line will curve to the right of the ball. Here we go; you just experienced the Coriolis effect.

CHAPTER SUMMARY

- Trajectory cannot be changed unless acted upon by an external force;
- The erratic trajectory of a balloon is caused by the air turbulence around the object, since there is a presence of air both inside and outside the object.
- Projectile motion is the trajectory an object takes as it moves in a parabola through the air, influenced by both vertical and horizontal motion.
- Vertical motion is influenced by the gravity acting upon it.
- Projectile motion describes an object's trajectory as it moves along a parabolic path through the air, caused by the combined effects of vertical and horizontal motions.
- The curved trajectory of some objects is called the Magnus effect. When the spin of a projectile creates pressure differences between the faster and slower object's sides.
- Objects of the same mass dropped from the same height will land simultaneously, whether dropped vertically or horizontally.
- The Coriolis effect is a result of Earth's rotation and influences the movement of objects, making their paths curve instead of going straight.

Friction

8

The construction of the pyramids and the wonders of ancient Egypt was no easy feat. For many years, modern civilization has been intrigued by how the ancient Egyptians managed to transport millions of rocks, such as limestone and granite, each weighing an average of 2.5 tons. In a study published in 2014 on the website *Physical Review Letters*,[1] physicists from the University of Amsterdam simulated how the ancient Egyptians dragged these massive rocks across the desert by wetting the sand and using sleds to slide them along.

This research clarifies the big questions and debunks many myths about how the rocks were transported to the sites where the pyramids were built. It provides a glimpse into the ingenuity of the ancient Egyptians and shows how a simple solution can solve one of humankind's greatest mysteries.

According to the research team, when dragging a sled through dry sand, they observed sand building up in front of it, requiring more force to keep the weight from moving. However, by making the sand wet—just enough to create a smoother surface with water particles between the grains—friction was reduced, and much less force was needed to pull the weight.

How fascinating is that? Without modern tools, the ancient Egyptians moved giant rocks by simply wetting the sand and altering its composition. Friction is truly fascinating!

Friction is a force that resists motion between two objects in contact, regardless of their composition.

It is crucial to understand the composition of materials when working on your animation, as each material has its own coefficient of friction. As observed with the naked eye, a smooth surface will have less friction than a rough one. However, it's important to note that even smoother surfaces have imperfections at the atomic level. When combined with the composition of the other object in contact, the results will vary.

In nature, friction is constantly present and may only be absent in some instances, such as in a vacuum. You may ask, if a vacuum is the absence of matter, why only in some instances? Even in a vacuum of space, matter exists in tiny amounts, such as atoms or gases. Therefore, a spaceship travelling through deep space, for example, could experience a small amount of friction when encountering this matter. However, this scenario is just an example. Space is unimaginably massive, and atoms and gases are so spread out that friction is rare and barely affects bodies in motion.

When discussing this topic, it's important for the animator to understand both static and kinetic friction, as both are crucial for achieving the best results for the animation.

DOI: 10.1201/9781003642824-8

8.1 STATIC FRICTION

In simple terms, static friction is the force that resists the initiation of motion when objects are at rest.

Imagine object A at rest, while object B attempts to move it. The frictional force of object A resists this motion, acting in the opposite direction of object B's push. As object B applies more force, object A will increase its static friction until the force exerted by object B exceeds the static frictional force of object A. The greater the mass of object A, the greater the frictional force, as its increased weight presses it harder against the surface, creating more contact points and increasing friction between the objects.

When observing a character pushing a box, the box starts moving slowly and speeds up. You might say, "That makes sense — Slow In and Slow Out[2]!" You're correct and thinking like an animator, which is excellent! However, the goal is to understand physics as you know animation. The box starts slowly because it is at rest, and a force greater than its mass is required to overcome static friction.

Slow In and Out also happens when we go from an idle pose to a walk, or when we raise our arms, for example. Force is required to move the arms from rest. Additionally, there is friction in our atmosphere because particles are held within it by gravity; furthermore, another significant factor in this movement is body mechanics, as controlled motion is a function of the brain to prevent injury.

Let me explain why this happens when kinetic friction is in action. When an object is at rest, or has zero acceleration, gravity and the object's mass are in action. As you apply a force to push or pull the object, the static friction will match that force, increasing continuously to keep the object at rest. The object begins to move when the static friction reaches its limit. If the force to pull or push the object remains the same, the speed is constant; if the force increases, the object accelerates. From that point on, kinetic friction takes over. However, if the force drops below the object's mass and friction, the object stops, reverting to static friction.

It is essential to consider static friction when planning and working on a new animation. If the character is moving an object, the animator should consider how heavy the object is, what the surface it will be dragged on looks like, what it is made of, and how much force the character is applying to oppose the static friction.

8.2 KINETIC FRICTION

Kinetic friction is the force that acts on moving objects to oppose their motion across a surface. Compared to static friction mentioned above, kinetic friction requires much less force to keep the objects in motion, since they already have momentum once they overcome static friction.

Have you ever tried moving a stalled car? I have experienced it a few times, and it can be rewarding to help someone in need or quite stressful when it happens to you. Using this example, when pushing a stalled car, the initial force must exceed the car's mass and the static friction; fortunately, the car has wheels, which help reduce friction. Once the motion begins, keeping it moving becomes easier and requires much less force; this is an example of kinetic friction. It is important to consider that, depending on the surface, mass, and external forces applied, the object can remain in motion for a shorter or longer period. However, the object will eventually come to rest, if no external force is applied or if the force applied is less than the mass and friction acting on it (Figure 8.1).

FIGURE 8.1 Image of a stalled car being pushed, showing static and kinetic friction.

8.3 ASPERITY

By looking at objects, they may appear smooth and without irregularities, but there are small fissures and deformations that, when in contact with other objects, create friction. These tiny, or even microscopic, deformations are called asperities. The greater the force between the objects, the more contact the tiny deformations will have with each other, creating more friction.

Deformation is the process in which a subject changes its shape under the exertion of pressure; naturally, the level of friction between objects is correlated with the applied force. We will be discussing a few practical examples you can use in animation.

If a character is standing idle or walking, it is natural for there to be a slight deformation of its feet from compression against the surface due to the character's weight and from constantly shifting the centre of mass. In most cases, the composition of feet or shoes isn't rigid; the skin or shoes will deform when weight is applied, at the moment of contact, and the pressure is released when the foot comes off the surface. I encourage my students to include this detail to bring their animation to the next level. It is crucial, however, not to exaggerate it. If no deformation is applied, the feet feel rigid and inflexible. On the other hand, if you over-exaggerate, the feet will feel floaty and drifty. There must be a balance.

With traditional 2D animation or handling very complex rigs in 3D animation, it is possible to have more control over muscle deformation. However, most character rigs do not possess the ability to create deformation at this level for all controls. In this case, intersecting the character with the environment, props, or itself will solve the problem and create a sense of compression on the skin, muscles, and clothing. This handy trick prevents the character from feeling rigid and as though it is floating against the environment, making the animation more natural and believable.

Consider asperity carefully in animation when objects interact, as the animator should create a convincing illusion for the audience. Always think about how much force is applied to produce a realistic sense of friction (Figure 8.2).

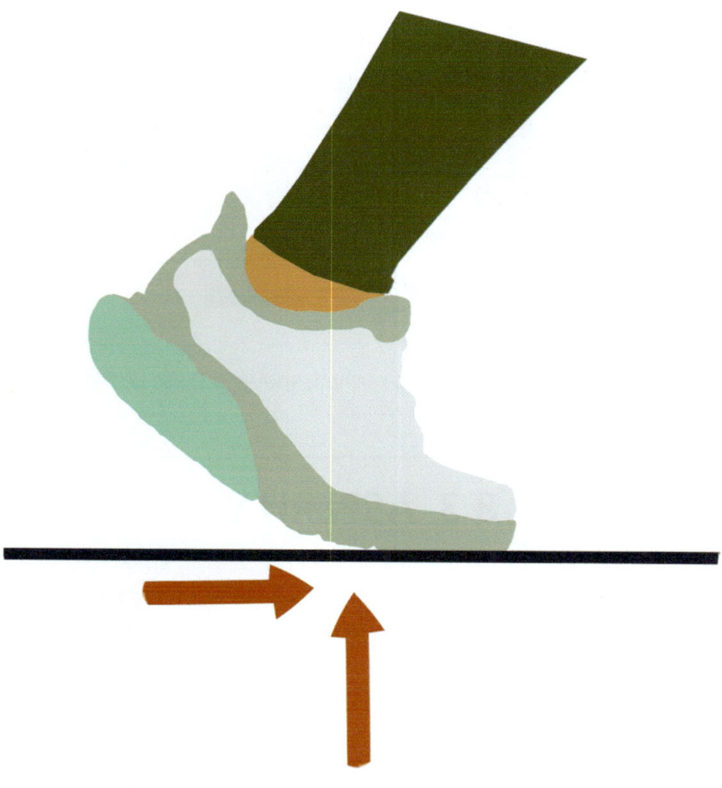

FIGURE 8.2 Image of a foot stepping with a trajectory with friction.

Unintentional sliding feet is a common mistake among new animators when working on character performances. It's natural here to focus on striking poses. However, sometimes the feet and legs can obstruct the animator's ability to achieve the desired pose, leading to adjustments in between. So, intending to focus on the key poses, the animator overlooks important moments where the feet should be planted to give the character stability. When the animation plays, the character feels weightless due to the constant sliding of the feet.

Experienced animators, with years of production experience and established workflows, are aware of potential issues when posing characters. Nevertheless, even they are not immune to sliding feet. Exhaustion, pressure to meet deadlines, and hours staring at the same animation can lead them to overlook these tasks.

As an animator, you should be able to review and direct your work, addressing any unnecessary motion (Figure 8.3).

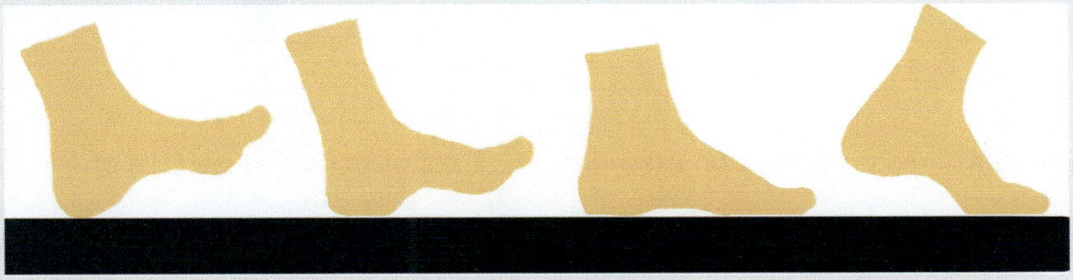

FIGURE 8.3 Image showing foot contact and its deformation.

Friction is crucial when discussing weight distribution for many animations you might encounter in your career. Starting with locomotion, we use our planted foot in the back to push us forward, using friction to provide enough grip to move at the speed we intend. As discussed earlier, asperities and weight are important to consider, but also the material and shape of the objects in contact. Bare feet on concrete will behave differently from dress shoes on ice.

The animator can effectively use friction when considering body mechanics, as humans constantly rely on it to perform various types of movements. For example, when we pivot on the ball of the foot to gain more distance. The absence of this body feature could lead to muscle and tendon injuries caused by excessive strain. As humans can only go as far as our bones and tendons allow, pivoting on the toes can provide an extra reach. It is easy to see this example when dancers or martial arts professionals use the same function, from their toes and friction, to move and cover wider distances. Imagine how disastrous a back kick would be without the friction from the toes pivoting under the person performing it (Figure 8.4).

Heels also serve a similar purpose, enabling us to pivot and distribute our weight in rare instances, such as turning on our axis or performing certain Tai Chi movements. In these instances, practitioners pivot on their heels, aiding in balance while maintaining their stance.

FIGURE 8.4 Image of a person executing a kick not pivoting and pivoting on the ball of the foot.

Although heels can also use friction to assist with pivoting, the most common pivot point in sports and everyday activities is the ball of the foot. The ball of the foot also helps absorb impact, acting like a vehicle suspension to prevent injuries to our bones and muscles.

Another essential function of the ball of the foot is to help us exert force for movement. We can use it to propel ourselves in different directions to initiate a walk, run, or evading motion, among other actions.

When dealing with props, friction constantly acts on the character and the object. Picture a warrior wielding a sword; the object has mass, a centre of gravity, and a surface that allows the character to grip. During a battle, the warrior will swing, hit, and slash. The handle, or hilt, is likely to provide a much more comfortable grip than the rest of the weapon, which is the opposite of comfort. The hilt can be made from various materials, such as leather, fabric, and, for traditional katanas, ray skin. The reason is to achieve better results while wielding the weapon. These materials were among the solutions found to improve grip due to their surfaces and textures. The last thing a warrior in a bloody and sweaty battle wants is their weapon to fly away because there isn't enough friction on the handle.

Studying real-life movement helps you better understand friction. Observe how dancers and athletes move on surfaces, using their feet to control the speed at which their bodies are launched; a stronger grip combined with a firm push can propel us much further and faster (Figure 8.5).

FIGURE 8.5 Image of a ballet dancer jumping.

CHAPTER SUMMARY

- Friction is a force that opposes motion between two objects in contact with each other.
- Changing the surface composition will influence how friction interacts between objects.
- Static friction is the force that resists the initiation of movement when objects are stationary; on the other hand, the kinetic force acts on moving objects, opposing their motion.
- Asperities are small or microscopic deformations on objects. As the force between them increases, these deformations come into closer contact, increasing friction.
- Even the smoothest surface to the naked eye will have imperfections at an atomic level.
- A common observation that is easy to spot is when humans use their toes or heels to pivot when performing weight shift, locomotion, and many other motions.
- Study the composition of objects to understand how friction will affect your animation.

NOTES

1 Van der Waals-Zeeman Institute, IoP, University of Amsterdam, Science Park 904, 1098XH Amsterdam, Netherlands; Institute for Advanced Studies in Basic Sciences, P.O. Box 45195-1159 Zanjan, Iran; Material Imaging, UR Navier, 77420 Champs-sur-Marne, France; Experimental Physics, Saarland University, D-66123 Saarbrücken, Germany; Gravitation Group, TATA Institute of Fundamental Research, 1 Homi Bhabha Road, 400005 Mumbai, India.
Sliding Friction on Wet and Dry Sand, https://journals.aps.org/prl/abstract/10.1103/PhysRevLett.112.175502.

2 Frank Thomas, Ollie Johnston, *The Illusion of Life*, *The Disney Animation* (1981).

Deformation

9

Have you ever asked what in the universe can be deformed? The answer may blow your mind. Theoretically speaking, everything in the universe can undergo deformation. Some may think that only objects containing mass can be deformed, but this is not the case. Even light, which is composed of photons, a massless particle of electromagnetic radiation, can be distorted through refraction, diffraction, and gravity. Let me break this down.

Refraction occurs when light travels through transparent objects, such as water or glass. When light passes through a transparent or translucent material, its path changes. You may have noticed that an object appears to change direction when it is partially submerged in water. We know that physical objects carrying mass are not bent per se just by being submerged; their structure doesn't change. However, light is what we see, and our vision results from light entering our eyes and being processed by our brains. In this scenario, the light is deformed (Figure 9.1).

Diffraction is somewhat different. In this context, light bends when it passes through corners or small apertures. You may have noticed that in a room, when the light comes from one direction, it will overshoot beyond the corner. Even in a dark room or cave with a tiny aperture through which light can pass, it spreads out, illuminating the area (Figure 9.2).

Another way light can undergo the deformation process is through the force of gravity. Einstein's General Relativity says that the entire fabric of spacetime can deform due to gravity, as seen in the first chapter. Observing the black hole accretion disc is an excellent example of how gravity can bend light. Black holes are regions in space where gravity is so intense that even light cannot escape, making them invisible to the naked eye and telescopes.

The point of no return is when an object crosses the event horizon. This region of a black hole is where nothing can escape, not even light. The event horizon appears as the dark boundary of a black hole, and, as mentioned earlier, our eyes can only see where there is light. Once an object crosses the event horizon, the escape velocity required exceeds the speed of light. Since nothing in the universe can travel faster than light, anything that crosses this boundary cannot return.

The event horizon can often be confused with the centre of the black hole, or in other words, the singularity. This region, in my opinion, is the most interesting part of a black hole, and it is located at the dead centre of it. It is the final destination of everything that passes through the event horizon. The curious thing is that nobody knows

DOI: 10.1201/9781003642824-9

FIGURE 9.1 Image of a pencil in a glass of water showing refraction.

what it actually is, and astronomers debate whether the singularity is a mathematical or physical structure.

The way scientists spot black holes and assess their mass can vary depending on the telescope used. The Hubble telescope observes matter around the black hole, such as gas and stars. Other telescopes, known as X-ray telescopes, use their lenses and technology to detect the temperature of objects surrounding the black hole. In summary, since the black hole cannot be seen, telescopes observe the accretion disc, consisting of particles orbiting the black hole. This disc creates the iconic image of a black hole, where gravity is so strong that light is bent around it.

In the previous chapter, we explored friction, including an example of animating a 3D character's feet. Depending on its technical limitations, you might not have enough controls for deformations. A trick is to slightly overshoot the contact, allowing the character to go through the surface to give some impression of deformation. You can use

FIGURE 9.2 Image of light shining through a corner.

this same trick in many situations where contact occurs, especially with props and the environment.

You might have noticed that in some video games, when a game character is sitting or interacting with objects, it feels as if the character floats and is as rigid as the objects. This can result from several factors, such as the character's limitations, a lack of controls, the project's budget, or even a technological deficiency. Resolving this issue, however, is not an impossible task. It's actually quite simple to overcome these limitations. In fact, it's easier and much cheaper to just intersect the character with the props and environment than to deal with deformation at this level.

At the end of the day, this comes down to two options, and it really depends on who is reviewing the animations. Some people don't like to see any intersection, and the animator will have to work around it, ensuring the poses and contact are true to reality. Others are fine with some intersection to make the work feel more natural. What I can say is, the first scenario rarely looks good.

In the example below, you can observe that the contact exists. However, the naturalness of a person sitting is not there. It delivers a sense of inflexibility that equals the object the character interacts with. If the character were to sit this way, it wouldn't feel relaxed, and the audience would notice that something is not right, as you have probably noticed when playing a game, for example (Figure 9.3).

FIGURE 9.3 Image of a character sitting with no deformation.

On the other hand, when the character slightly intersects with the object, the animation would be much more natural and relaxed. It is much easier for the audience to relate to this character, which feels natural, than to see a floaty, rigid one (Figure 9.4).

In the following example, you can see a character holding a prop. An inexperienced animator may leave many gaps to prevent the hand and fingers from intersecting with the object, creating fewer friction points and making the object feel loose, without deforming as naturally as a human hand would. Deformation is not only a natural process resulting from our body's composition, but it also leads to stronger contact and grip through friction (Figure 9.5).

In the following example, you can see that with a slight intersection, you can achieve a more natural feeling in your character's grip. When it comes to the freedom of drawing, it is much easier to show deformation without intersecting. Although it may sound counterintuitive at first, intersection used with caution in a 3D environment can yield a similar result. I encourage you to try it out; you will see how much more believable the animation looks. A good experiment you can try now is to grab an object or even your other wrist. The first time, imagine you are a 3D character and do your best

FIGURE 9.4 Image of a character sitting with deformation.

FIGURE 9.5 Image of a character holding a prop with no deformation.

to avoid intersecting your body at the point of contact; you will notice that the grip feels loose and weak. Next, hold a little tighter and observe the skin deforming for a stronger grip; this feels more robust and grounded.

If you have ever experienced working with a character rig, you will know what I'm talking about. The rigs generally lack the control to deform like our bodies or the freedom of a drawing; the character can even pass through its own mesh. Your goal is to know when to find the perfect balance between what constitutes a weak contact and what indicates a visible intersection (Figure 9.6).

FIGURE 9.6 Image of a character holding a prop with deformation.

9.1 DEFORMING FORCE

Elastic and plastic deformation, often referred to as inelastic deformation, represent two distinct types of deformation. The object's composition and the external force applied to it play a key role in determining which type is at work.

Elastic deformation occurs when a force is applied to an object and then released, causing it to return to its original shape.

Can you imagine a practical example where elastic deformation could affect a character you are animating? Assuming the intention in your character is to replicate a human body, there should be many.

In the examples above, I mentioned that there is deformation when your character is dealing with props or the environment. However, when the character stops interacting with the prop or environment, the objects will return to their original shape.

On the other hand, plastic deformation refers to a type of deformation that cannot be undone once the applied force is removed.

In animation, plastic deformation can be observed when an irreversible change occurs in your character or object, ranging from the destruction of a wall or building to an indentation in an inflexible object to a broken bone. All of these are considered deformations, and the consequences will vary depending on the desired composition you are aiming for in your story.

In nature, anything can undergo deformation as long as the conditions are suitable.

Fluids, such as water or air, are constantly changing shape. The ocean continuously deforms under the moon's gravity. Water in a bottle takes the shape of the bottle until you pour it into a glass, at which point it takes the shape of the glass. Air can change shape simply by raising your hand and waving; even before waving, slightly moving your arm will alter its shape.

Harder materials, such as iron and rocks, are also affected by deformation. When heat or pressure is applied, iron combined with carbon forms steel, which can be bent multiple times and reshaped to create objects such as a katana, the famous Japanese sword. When rocks are melted at temperatures between approximately 700°C and 1300°C, they turn into magma, permanently changing their shape even after cooling.

Diamonds, the most rigid material on Earth, can deform plastically. This process permanently changes the diamond, even if only on an atomic scale.

Squash and stretch are the most effective examples of how deformation affects a character. Ignoring or misusing it will result in non-realistic animation; therefore, it is essential first to understand your object's composition. This will give you the first clue to determine if the deformations affecting it will be irreversible. With that in mind, you can assess the second aspect: the external forces acting on the object. I like to start with gravity, and to simplify, let's go with this one for the following example:

Assume you want to work on a walk cycle. You have the poses and the timing, and for the next pass, you want to add some flair to make it look natural. Gravity on its own will not have much influence without a surface; otherwise, the character would be in a state of freefall. Since this is a walk cycle, we need a surface, making it a second external factor affecting your character.

You can determine how your character's body will react by using the knowledge acquired in this chapter. For example, with each step a human takes during a walk, about 1.5 times their body weight is exerted on the foot, making deformation impossible to ignore.

A character with greater mass experiences more reaction force when in contact with a surface. For example, as they walk, an elephant's ankles and paws absorb all their weight against gravity and the contact surface, creating deformation. This results in a ripple effect throughout the body, deforming areas with higher concentrations of skin and muscle. In comparison, consider a healthy cat walking; although its body also deforms, the concentration of mass is much lower than that of an elephant. It is crucial to consider the character's composition, environment, and type of animation beforehand, so your search for references and the final result feel natural and accurate.

In production, based on my experience with gameplay and cinematic animation, it is often necessary to be creative to convey the sense of deformation when it comes to limited characters lacking in extra controls for muscle deformation and other elements that can be used to add more flavour to the animation. Slightly intersecting the character when interacting with props and the environment, exaggerating overlap and overshoot when you can to simulate clothes or props physics or in a more complex way, using facial controls to deform the character's face upon a hit are examples on how you can push the character for a more compelling result.

Deformation is something we need to be creative with to achieve and convey the feeling of impact to the player. A direct hit, such as a punch, ripples from the area of impact, where the force is greater and deforms the target for a short period, while the force is distributed and absorbed by the body. A hit on a character's face will have a different result than a hit on the same character's torso. As in the example above, this depends on skin, muscle, fat, and joint concentration.

By observing references of a fighting competitor being hit in the face, it becomes easier to track the impact area through trajectory and deformation. The area of impact is the one with the most significant deformation, and since the jaw is very mobile, it visibly reacts to the force. The tissues around are no different; however, at some point, the energy is lost. That is why the entire body will not deform to a concentrated hit like a punch. However, remember that it depends on the area of effect: The larger the area, the greater the deformation.

Now, you are an animator. What can you do to make this animation believable and natural? The first step is to understand the character motivations.

Your character's backstory is a great starting point to guide you through the animation process. As a storyteller, you can create a document to tell a short story for this character. Things like: Identity, motivations and moral code are a good start when developing a character for your story. Next, thinking on the art delivery, if the story and characters are based in realism or not will influence how you should look for reference and animating the characters. A story based in realism will be limited for some of the physics laws, otherwise it may appear disconnected from reality. However, if your story is not grounded in reality, for example, the cartoon Atom Ant,[1] where the hero is a tiny ant fighting much larger enemies. Ants are known for their strength, but Atom Ant is a superhero who is much stronger than a regular ant. He used to throw and punch these villains effortlessly, breaking the sense of reality. However, this freedom is based on the style and story, making the work somewhat easier to explore.

A realistic animation, in which I have more experience in the industry, is heavily based on real-life movement and the influence of physics. As mentioned before, we should be careful about how much freedom we aim for in the animation before breaking the characters and realism. By understanding the story and characters, we can use the controls provided by the rigging team as tools to convey the impact and ripple effect of the hit. Having a knowledge of physics, acceleration, trajectory, and, of course, having a good reference, I'm sure your results will be satisfactory (Figure 9.7).

The human body is composed of tissues, organs, cells, etc. It is expected to deform under stress. Shifting your weight on a chair will deform the area under pressure in your body. In fact, the simple action of being seated on a chair deforms the area in contact with the object—that's natural! Imagine applying much more tension to the body; even through facial expressions, the facial muscles are deformed. I encourage you to observe

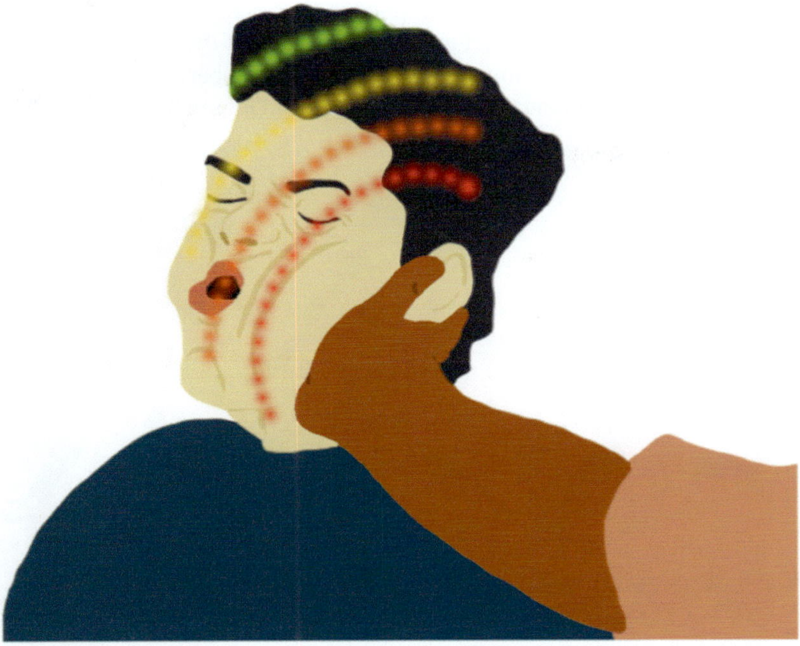

FIGURE 9.7 Image of a person getting slapped and the ripple effect.

how much the face communicates through non-verbal cues and micro-expressions; you can learn much from them.

A great example of object deformation I like to use in class is when a batter makes contact with the bat and a baseball. Picture this: Just as the bat strikes the ball, everything happens so quickly that it's hard to see any change. To the naked eye, the ball seems to maintain its shape. However, in reality, the ball distorts momentarily. Due to its composition and the sheer opposite force exerted by the bat, the elastic deformation that was once applied loses its energy since there is no more contact with the bat. The ball quickly returns to its spherical shape as it is launched.

Now, I encourage you to try this experiment in your animation software or even a drawing. First, animate the ball without deformation and see how it plays out. You will notice something feels off, as if the animation is stiff. Try this instead: Stretch the ball slightly before the bat makes contact. This will cause the ball to deform into a more oval shape, stretching towards the bat. When the bat strikes the ball, squash it—it does not have to be too extreme and exaggerated if you do not want to. It's all about finding the right feel and the result you're aiming for. After the ball is released, it will briefly stretch once again into an oval shape, but soon, it will return to its spherical form. You could also slightly curve the bat before the impact for a more exaggerated feeling. There is no right or wrong; it depends on how stylized you want your animation to be.

By getting the timing, poses, deformation, and trajectory right, it does not matter if it is stylized or realistic. The intention of your animation is clear, and the chances of achieving a natural, great shot that captures the essence of deformation and motion are high.

As you can see, deformation can be applied to almost any animation, and the extent to which you can push it will depend on the composition of the character or object and how stylized you want your animation to appear. Remember to observe how things deform around you and continually seek out references (Figure 9.8).

FIGURE 9.8 Image of a baseball deforming upon contact with the bat.

CHAPTER SUMMARY

- Even light, which is composed of photons, a massless particle, can undergo the process of deformation through refraction, diffraction, and gravity.
- Intersecting characters with props and environment will deliver a sense of deformation to it and make the animation feel natural.
- Consider the environment and the character's composition, mass, and speed at which they interact in order to plan how deformation will affect them.
- Elastic deformation happens when a force is applied to an object and then removed, allowing it to bounce back to its original shape.
- Plastic deformation is a form of deformation that cannot be reversed after the force is taken away.
- Consider the area of impact the deformation will ripple through the character, and the force and velocity of the projectile that will be in contact with it.
- The amount of deformation in your animation will always depend on the material's composition, mass, and speed.

NOTE

1 *Atom Ant*, Hanna-Barbera (1965).

Overshoot 10

Have you ever noticed that when a vehicle stops, it moves slightly forward and then back as it comes to a complete stop? And, if you're inside a one, whether as a passenger, driver, or pilot, when it stops, it not only maintains its forward momentum slightly, but everyone else inside also experiences the same motion. This results from objects, whether inside or outside the vehicle, being transported by the vehicle, which tend to resist changes in their state of motion. In physics, this is due to inertia; in animation, it is called overshoot. In other words, the objects in motion will maintain their state of motion until an external force or the object's limitations interrupt their trajectory. Once this happens, the object in motion will maintain its trajectory, slightly pass its target point, and settle until all its energy is lost.

This happens with almost anything that moves to a stop. In animation, overshoot is often used as follow-through and refers to movement beyond the target position before settling into rest. Humans and animals are excellent references; joints, tissues, and limbs are all connected, and there is always a reaction to the action of motion. With a constantly shifting centre of mass and all the moving parts, every subtle movement our bodies make involves an overshoot. Start observing it, and you will see.

At the stop of a walk or run, for example, there's no immediate halt; the energy maintains its momentum, and due to several factors, such as body mechanics, balance, and shifts in the centre of mass, the body has to adjust to reach the desired and comfortable resting pose.

A great example is when someone lands from a jump: To avoid damaging knees and joints, we absorb the impact by bending and using our leg muscles to soften the landing. If possible, you can try it yourself. Stand up and jump. Naturally, your knees will bend when you contact the surface to soften the landing. The higher the jump, the lower you will get, as your joints and muscles will have a greater force to absorb. This impact ripples through the entire body. Since the body wants to be in motion, it falls constantly, but is interrupted by the surface. The limbs react to the impact, causing them to overshoot as the body comes to rest (Figure 10.1).

DOI: 10.1201/9781003642824-10

FIGURE 10.1 Image of a character jumping, overshooting, and settling.

10.1 THE FIVE PRINCIPLES OF OVERSHOOT

Overshooting is a direct response to motion and cannot occur without it; however, motion can exist without overshooting. There are several ways a character can overshoot from motion, and how you decide to have it in your animation will directly result from observing the following aspects, which I like to call the five principles of overshoot: Pivots, Acceleration, Trajectory, Mass, and Composition.

Pivots will help visualize where the connections and points where the object will bend under stress are; Acceleration will determine the speed of the object before it stops; Trajectory will help you identify where the object comes from and where it should go when overshooting; Mass relates to the object's weight and how much force is needed to stop it; finally, Composition refers to what the object is made of. It seems quite a lot, but don't worry, once you get the idea, everything will be clearer (Figure 10.2).

Bear in mind that there is no specific order for the five principles; each serves as a guide for the animator to understand how the object should be animated and which references to use.

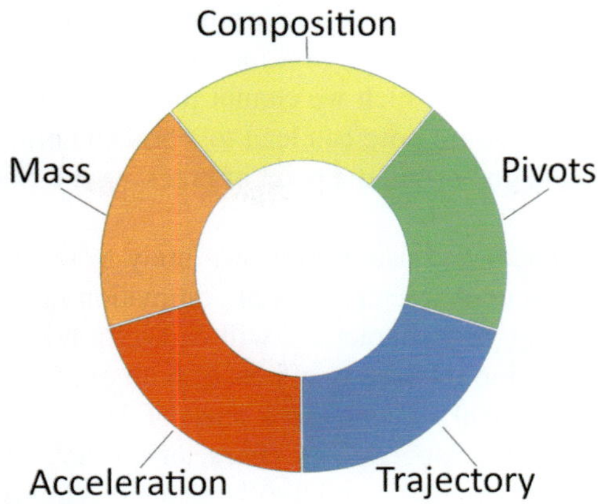

FIGURE 10.2 Image of the five principles of overshoot.

10.2 PIVOTS

Pivots are mobile areas where an object can move naturally without breaking. In other words, they are points of least resistance, like joints. One example of a pivot is the elbow.

Elbows can only rotate on one axis, and they can only perform rotation in other directions, such as near or farther from the torso, because the shoulder drives the movement (Figure 10.3).

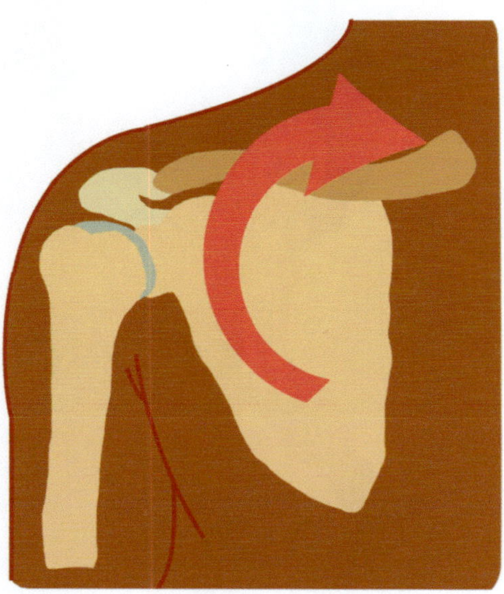

FIGURE 10.3 Image of a shoulder rotation pattern.

For a character, it is essential to have a strong understanding of anatomy to animate overshoot effectively. Whether you are working on a human or a creature, the body has physiological limits beyond which we cannot push; the same should apply to the animated character. An awkward pose can lead to a broken animation. Unless the animation style allows you to go beyond the point of breaking the character's limbs, make sure to use this carefully.

By observing references and using your own body to simulate motion, you will understand the limits of your character. After all, animation references real life. In the animation context, rotating your character, I will call it, in negative, beyond its limits of hyperextension, can lead to interesting effects of both overlap and overshoot. These results can represent a powerful reaction and a sense of flexibility in the character.

How much you decide to exaggerate the character's overshoot depends on the style you are looking for in your animation and the character's technical limitations.

Realistic animations are more restrictive than cartoonish ones; if you aim to enhance appeal with more overshoot, you must base your work in real life and exaggerate from there.

However, be aware that pushing the character too much in a negative direction will make your animation unrealistic and the character broken, as shown in Figure 10.4.

FIGURE 10.4 Image of a leg unrealistic overshoot.

The same idea applies to inanimate objects that you might eventually animate. A door hinge is a good example; it provides direction and limits how much the door can open and close, similar to a joint. Without the hinge, the door would have no restrictions on where it can go or where it can pivot. So, how can you animate a door slam with overshoot, since a hinge and the door frame limit its overshoot? In this second scenario, you are relying only on the reaction force and a few more details.

You could hold the pose at its maximum range for a couple of frames to convey momentum. During this time, you can add some tiny back-and-forth motion that will represent the force of the door slam until the door comes to rest.

Reaction force occurs when an object reaches its range limits or is abruptly interrupted, and it can only move in directions other than the previous trajectory. This triggers a reaction due to the interruption of motion, acceleration, and the object's composition.

10.3 ACCELERATION

The rule of acceleration applies to everything in motion. Mass, gravity, and fluids are just a few elements that can drastically change how objects accelerate. However, not only do external factors come into play when considering acceleration, but the object may also possess energy to accelerate, such as an engine or muscles.

The acceleration of an object, along with the other four principles, will determine how much overshoot an object will have when it comes to a stop. It is essential to note that the action of constant acceleration does not overshoot until the object comes to a stop.

Overshoot results directly from an object's acceleration while in motion. To clarify, consider this example: Hold an object with your arms relaxed by your side, and walk a few steps before stopping. Notice how far the arm holding the object swings. Now, instead of walking, run a few meters with the same object and then stop. You'll observe that your arm overshoots much further.

For a better understanding of how acceleration can change the outcome of the animation, let's compare two objects being dropped from a building. First, take a US 50-cent coin, which weighs 11.340 g[1] as I write this book. If this coin is dropped from a building, it is unlikely anyone will be seriously injured by it due to air resistance and the object's shape. Of course, you could expect some minor injuries to the person hit by the coin and potential criminal charges, so please refrain from doing so. On the other hand, a 9 mm calibre bullet weighs exactly 9.52544 g. The chances of a 9 mm bullet fired by a gun causing harm or worse to someone are much higher compared to a slightly heavier coin dropped from a building, due to the projectile's acceleration.

It is important to consider the story you are telling, so the next step is to research, plan, and determine how the objects will accelerate, whether through their propulsion or external factors. Characteristics such as the object's shape, its story (why does this object move at this speed), external influences, and references are vital tools for enhancing your animation and, consequently, the overshoot.

10.4 TRAJECTORY

From what we observed in the projectile motion in Chapter 7, we know that an object in motion cannot be interrupted without an external force acting upon it. The same applies to an object about to overshoot. Due to inertia, the character or object will attempt to maintain its state of motion, which directly opposes any external force that tries to stop it. For example, if you take a pendulum from its resting position and drop it from one axis, without any other external factors affecting it, it will move straight to the opposite side. On its own, the pendulum is limited to the string's length and the bob's mass. Still, independently of its anatomy, once the object is in motion on one axis, it will keep swinging on this same axis until it stops, unless, of course, it is affected by any external force that will change its trajectory. We understand that gravity naturally pulls the object, and the pendulum will descend farther with each swing. As gravity pulls the pendulum down, it continues to move because it has mass. When the object is released, the gravitational pull accelerates the bob downwards, and its pivot and string are the only points of contact between the bob and the ground. With no other external factors acting upon the object, the only trajectory is along one axis until the pendulum comes to a state of rest.

The example of a pendulum is much simpler than that of a character with several pivots and unpredictability. Let's say in your story, a character is running and, without noticing, hits a wall. If your character does not notice, you know that the acceleration will be constant, so there will be no slowdown. At the moment of contact, the character cannot hit every part of its body at once; ultimately, this decision is yours. Every run can be different, and each character can have its own identity and personality. As the storyteller, it is up to you to decide. However, if your character were to hit the wall at the same time, it would definitely not be any pose of a run but some very weird pose instead. The overshoot in a situation of running and hitting a wall is most commonly observed in the body parts that contact the object after the character is interrupted by it. Suppose the head is the first to hit the wall; at this moment, the head may overshoot to exaggerate or deform. This may not be very visible to the audience, but its absence can make the movement feel weak and weightless. Nonetheless, the larger motions are what give the audience a sense of force. As the head stops, the rest of the body continues in motion, causing the limbs and remaining parts to eventually hit the wall and come to a stop. Think about what should be overshooting in this scenario, depending on the run style of the character.

Consider the previous principles; acceleration determines how much your character overshoots. The pivots guide how the body rotates and reacts upon impact. This is followed by the last pose before contact and then the trajectory the character is following.

If your character is running in a straight line, for example, the trajectory is straight forward. The character cannot simply go from a straight run to an upward motion, at least not entirely.

From the same example, the torso and hip carry mass and determine direction, respectively, so they should remain straight to maintain their motion. However, arms and legs can overshoot upwards. Remember the pendulum example? These limbs hang from their pivots, so it is natural for them to swing upwards. Of course, the wall will stay there immobile, limiting the continuity of the motion, so keep that in mind (Figure 10.5).

FIGURE 10.5 Image of a character hitting a wall.

10.5 MASS

Mass can be confused with composition; however, a good way to tell them apart is to remember that mass is the amount of matter in an object, while composition refers to what that object is made of. For example, the human body can have different masses due to variations in bone density, muscle, and fat, among other factors. On the other hand, everyone's body is composed of the same elements, such as water, carbon, oxygen, hydrogen, and many others. Even light, which is a massless wave and particle, is made of photons.

Now that the difference between mass and composition is clear, let's break this down.

If you have a scenario where two objects with different masses are pushed with the same force, what would you say about which object should be faster? This answer depends on where this is happening. If, in this scenario, both objects are affected by the same gravitational field, the object with greater mass will move more slowly. However, it is essential to note that the weight of an object on our planet differs from its weight on the Moon or Jupiter, for instance.

From the example above, when external forces stop objects travelling at a faster speed, it will naturally undergo a greater overshoot because their masses experiences a greater acceleration.

It is essential to consider the mass and composition of the object resisting the other object's motion, and whether it is at rest or in motion. A playground ball rolling towards a wall at the same speed as it rolls towards another ball will have two very distinct outcomes when it comes to overshoot.

10.6 COMPOSITION

In composition, the material the object is made of and why it is vital when considering overshooting.

Everything in the known universe has a composition, except for the singularity of a black hole, and scientists still do not have an answer for that.

The singularity, which is at the centre of a black hole, is described as an area of infinite mass but zero volume. It still contains the mass of the collapsed object, but it has no composition. Since we cannot see past the event horizon, we may never discover the answer. However, a recent theory even suggests that our universe exists inside a black hole.[2]

When analysing the object you will animate, the composition plays a crucial role in determining how it will react to motion, whether on its own or in response to other factors.

For instance, if you animate three balloons—one filled with air, the other with water, and the last with sand—they will all have different responses when overshooting. The balloon remains the same, but we changed its composition by adding different materials. This answer sounds simple; you would know that the balloons are going to be animated and move very differently; however, this is just one example of infinite scenarios you will encounter as an animator.

Since motion is necessary for overshoot, all five principles should be considered, as neglecting any of them can affect the quality of your final product. Most of your work will require overshoot, so ensure you consider all factors, not only those related to the object but also those around it.

Overshoot is vital in animation because it conveys the feeling of mass and acceleration when an object comes to a stop. In real life, the reasons are no different; they occur, and we often don't even notice, as it's something we all experience. That is why I believe

Overshoot is not limited to humans and animals; machines, such as robots and vehicles, can also be influenced by it under certain conditions. It can be easy to take into consideration the biological features acting on us and apply the overshoot once you study the character's anatomy; however, if you take the time to understand the inanimate object you are about to animate, it becomes easy to grasp how overshoot has to be applied to it, since the laws of physics also affect them.

many animators tend to ignore overshoot, resulting in animations that feel weightless and unconvincing.

Without the reaction, the animation feels light and weak. Imagine a big T. rex rushing forward and then stopping. Even with proper timing and other animation fundamentals, without an overshoot, it will still lack a sense of weight and acceleration when this massive dinosaur stops, making it feel weightless and stiff.

For this reason, we add the overshoot to convey a strong reaction to the action of a massive creature transitioning to an idle animation. The same example applies to a big truck and a small car when they come to a halt. Comparing the two vehicles, the larger one requires more energy from its brakes' friction and overshoots more than a smaller car (Figure 10.6).

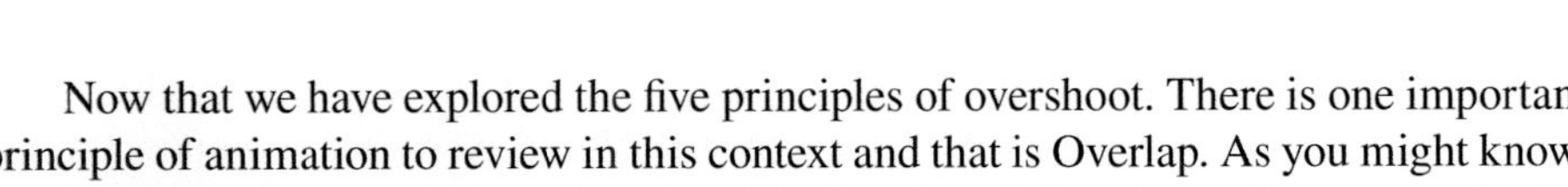

FIGURE 10.6 Image of a car stopping and overshooting.

Now that we have explored the five principles of overshoot. There is one important principle of animation to review in this context and that is Overlap. As you might know, overlap action is one of the principles of animation. When the animator breaks the character's momentum into parts to achieve smoothness and continuity, this approach is ideal for combining with overshoot, giving your animation a sense of realism. However, overshoot can also exist without overlapping action.

In other words, everything that overlaps overshoots, but not everything that overshoots overlaps. Let me show you a few more examples (Figure 10.7).

Now imagine a character with one bionic metal arm that is much heavier than the other. Your character runs, then stops for an idle animation. By using all five principles of overshoot, you should examine: the trajectory from where the character is running and stopping; the pivots and all the joints connecting the limbs; the acceleration of the running character, whether jogging or sprinting; the mass and composition of the two

FIGURE 10.7 Image of a hair overlapping and overshooting.

arms for reference. When the character stops, the overshoot on the heavier arm is less noticeable when compared to the other arm, since its mass is more influenced by inertia.

It is important to note that a heavy object tends to resist changes in its state of motion, as much as the overshoot tends to be much smaller compared to a lighter object. Stopping a heavy object once it is in motion requires more energy and time; this causes an offset in the animation, making the limbs settle at different times.

In a different scenario, picture an object with no pivots, just a single piece of material, like a wooden board, for the sake of this example. The material has no pivots; it is a single piece of wood cut into a square or rectangular shape. Let's say this object is launched towards a much harder and immobile object. Now that you know the five principles of overshoot, you need to put them all together to plan your animation.

Let's imagine a scenario where pivot is taken out of the equation. A plank is travelling towards another object. Since it is a single piece of wood, how can you overshoot this piece of material? There are several possibilities, depending on the other four elements of the principles and how the story is told. By knowing the object's mass, composition, trajectory, and acceleration, you already have some answers for this animation. What else should you ask? Where is this object hitting the target? What does the target look like, and is it made of? Let's use the image in Figure 10.8 for reference and imagine how you can overshoot this plank.

In the example above, the piece of plank is about to hit a heavy, steel, wrecking ball.

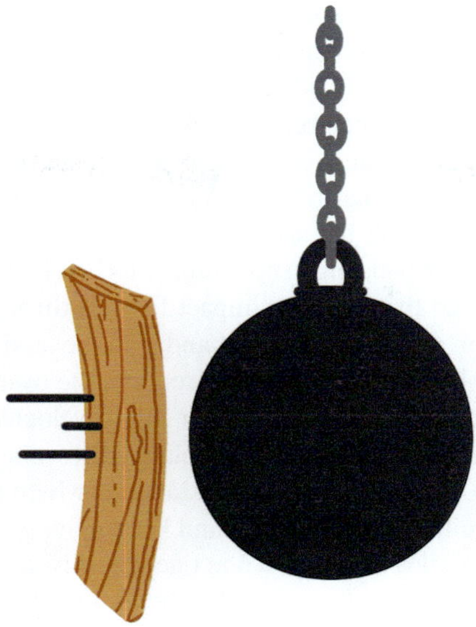

FIGURE 10.8 Image of a plank about to hit a wrecking ball.

Now, supposing the plank is following a straight trajectory towards the wrecking ball and will contact at its centre at an incredible velocity, how can you overshoot it? (Figure 10.9)

FIGURE 10.9 Image of a plank snapping upon contact with a wrecking ball.

In the first scenario, the overshoot can be the plank's least point of resistance, the breaking point. This is due to its composition: a somewhat hard yet weaker object compared to a solid steel wrecking ball, which slams into it at an incredible velocity. Since the contact occurs at the plank's centre, its weakest area, it would not be unusual to see it snap on contact. Remember that overshoot can also be an object's breaking point.

Let's analyse the second scenario to understand how the plank can react differently when it comes into contact with the wrecking ball. Suppose your plank isn't moving at an incredible velocity, or you might not want it to break. Another effective way to illustrate the overshoot and the resulting impact force is through the slight bending of the object. The animation will still overshoot and give the audience the impression you intend. By curving the plank in the opposite direction, the overshoot creates a sense of a sudden change in acceleration, from whatever initial velocity you have to an instant zero at the contact point, where the rest of the plank still wants to continue its forward motion. In this scenario, the point of least resistance is where it contacts the wrecking ball, allowing the extremities to remain free and keep moving forward.

As shown in the examples above, you don't necessarily need to do one or the other; there are several scenarios, but it is essential to break the questions down to make the most of your animation (Figure 10.10).

FIGURE 10.10 Image of a plank bending upon contact with a wrecking ball.

In some specific cases, overshoot cannot exist. When precision is necessary, and overshoot can lead to expensive or serious consequences, this is the case for a device like the osmometer, a measuring instrument used in laboratories, for research, and in industrial settings. This device cannot experience overshoot because its mechanics prevent it; any overshoot would compromise its accuracy.

Understanding the difference between overshoot and reaction force is also crucial, as they are often confused but are distinct aspects of physics and animation. Overshoot refers to the response or reaction where a motion exceeds its target value due to an object's momentum; meanwhile, the reaction or bounce force is the equal and opposite force between two objects when they interact, as in the example of a bouncing ball, as seen in Chapter 5 and more in Chapter 13.

CHAPTER SUMMARY

- Overshoot happens because an object in motion tends to continue moving, causing it to slightly pass the resting position before stopping.
- Overshoot cannot exist without motion, but motion can exist without overshoot.
- The five principles of overshoot are Pivots, Acceleration, Trajectory, Mass, and Composition.
- Faster objects will have a tendency to overshoot more than slower ones.
- The trajectory in which an object is travelling will determine where it should go when overshooting.
- The concept of mass is relative, and it depends on the setting in which your animation takes place.
- Mass indicates the amount of matter in an object, whereas composition describes what the object is made of.
- Everything that overlaps overshoots, but not everything that overshoots overlaps.

NOTES

1 Coin Specifications (2025) – https://www.usmint.gov/learn/coins-and-medals/circulating-coins/coin-specifications?srsltid=AfmBOorF6onPrPvLOWthuZZyjeAJ04bEP8tDA3Hh0nCqILs6a4mD1Hge.

2 Enrique Gaztanaga (2025) – https://www.port.ac.uk/news-events-and-blogs/blogs/space-cosmology-and-the-universe/what-if-the-big-bang-wasnt-the-beginning-our-research-suggests-it-may-have-taken-place-inside-a-black-hole.

Physics of Locomotion 11

Locomotion has been fundamentally linked to living organisms since life first appeared on Earth. An organism, using its means to generate energy and moving from one point to another, regardless of the mechanics and physiology, is an aspect of locomotion.

Locomotion is usually linked to walking or running, as we'll explore in this chapter; however, locomotion extends beyond walking or running—moving from one point to another through crawling, flying, swimming, and so on, are all forms of locomotion.

Some video game projects are so massive that they require an entire team of animators focused solely on locomotion. This is understandable. Modern games are so expensive and complex to develop that not only do humans with various archetypes and personalities need locomotion on all kinds of surfaces, but also creatures that fly, swim, or crawl. When building the game's move tree, it is important to remember that locomotion is integral to this system. The move tree is a visual representation of all possible movements and situations a character can have, and how everything blends from one motion to another to prevent the character from breaking when connecting animations are played.

Locomotion, like all animated movements, must have a reason and should appear believable. For example, a character can start moving by using friction from the surface to stay in motion. The reason they continue moving involves a combination of factors outlined in this book, such as friction, Newton's third law of motion, and balance, along with body mechanics and physiological aspects that generate motion in the human body.

Imagine you have a character who needs to travel from point A to point B, but along the way, this character must: sneak behind enemies in stealth mode, walking carefully; then jump from one platform to another; climb several walls; fight enemies while dodging their attacks; then jump into the water, swimming to the other side; and finally reach their goal.

In the example above, locomotion was executed directly or indirectly in every single step of the game, blending with various other animations. To give you a visual, next time you play a game, everything controlled by the left stick of a controller or the traditional WASD keys on a keyboard will most likely be for character locomotion.

DOI: 10.1201/9781003642824-11

Friction is a crucial aspect of locomotion because it provides the thrust for a push, while the surface pushes back in the opposite direction. Naturally, the other factors above should be considered when assessing locomotion; however, the absence of friction is directly related to the lack of motion itself.

When land creatures and humans move, their main source of propulsion is friction generated by their limbs against a surface. Flying creatures can utilize their anatomy to generate lift and thrust through their wings. They use a combination of lift from the flaps of their wings and drag from friction with the air.

Friction also provides the thrust that allows sea creatures to move; many species living in water use their bodies to push against the water, and others living on the ocean floor can push against the seabed.

The diagram below illustrates the primary forces involved in locomotion. For a character or object to move from one point to another, either friction or a push must occur for it to be considered locomotion. These forces can act independently or together; however, the absence of both prevents the movement from being considered locomotion. In such cases, motion can only happen through external influences.

As you can observe, from a simple locomotion, where the object moves from point A to B, friction and force are the main supporting forces. In either real life or animation, motion can be achieved by both of the forces shown in the diagram. Some other secondary responses are necessary for the locomotion to feel real; however, ignoring friction and push will result in issues that will ripple to the other responses. For example, a character moves quickly by generating more friction and force against the surface. At some point, the energy becomes momentum, and less of both is necessary, as you observe in a run, for instance. The legs are responsible for pushing and creating thrust, which then causes the rest of the body to respond, such as leaning slightly forward and swinging the arms vigorously. These movements are a consequence of the push.

If you use the same scenario but with less friction, the character will slide, and the energy will seem lost. Not having the body leaning forward and the arms swinging might make it feel as though something is missing, but the timing and the intention are still there. With just a few adjustments, you can add more personality to the character (Figure 11.1).

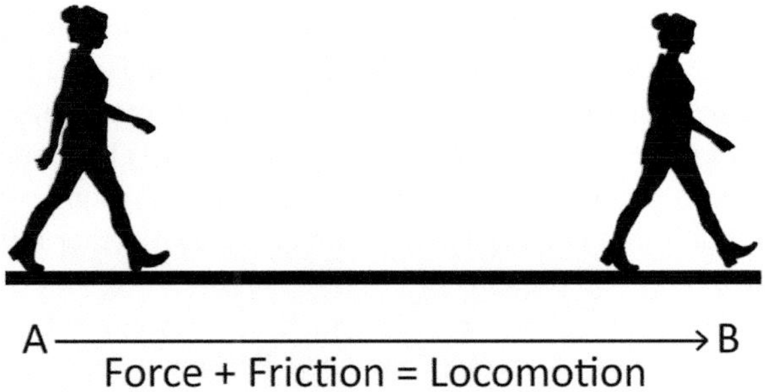

FIGURE 11.1 Image of the locomotion diagram.

If the diagram above reminds you of something we discussed in this book, you're right, the third law of motion is the best example to describe locomotion.

Another aspect of locomotion is mechanical locomotion, where machines move either under human control or through programming to operate independently. Examples include planes, rockets, and cars that start moving by burning fuel, as well as humanoid robots, which are either controlled by a person or designed to perform tasks autonomously. However, since these examples can be considered locomotion and are worth briefly mentioning in this book, I will focus on the organic type of locomotion.

Remember to consider and apply the fundamentals described above when animating a character's locomotion. By applying this knowledge, your animation will feel more grounded and significantly more appealing.

11.1 WALKING AND RUNNING

In *The Animator's Survival Kit*, by Richard Williams, the author says that when we walk, "We're going through a series of controlled falls."[1] Having heard this quote from one of my college teachers and eventually having had the chance to read the book, I did not fully agree with the statement. How can we be constantly falling as we walk? This idea has stuck with me for years. After examining several locomotion animations, observations, and research, I understand what the author intended to convey, but I still disagree with this statement in part. That said, I am by no means trying to dismiss the author's opinion or his contributions to animation, and I strongly encourage anyone to read the book and see the remarkable work Richard Williams has done throughout his career. Saying that we are controlling falls as we walk is the same as assuming everything involving motion is a controlled fall. The mechanics of locomotion are basically moving from one point to another and applying push through friction, as in walking, running, jumping, and even swimming. Isn't everything that moves doing the same thing all the time?

I would, in fact, add to what Richard Williams said and say that we are constantly controlling falls. As I write this book now, sitting in a chair, the object is preventing me from falling, and if it weren't for it, I would collapse to the floor. If I stand up for a stretch and my legs fail during a weight shift, I fall. While walking, I use my balance and contact with other objects to prevent falling. Locomotion isn't different; we are balanced constantly, and our weight is distributed to support that balance, along with the push from our legs against the surface. If someone falls during locomotion, it's due to an obstacle, an irregularity on the surface, an external factor, or even tangled legs. Falling from locomotion is simply a consequence of motion, like any other fall, because we are in a constant state of controlled falls.

What can be said about quadrupeds? Do you think they control falls when walking or running? Of course! They also remain balanced, fighting to remain in this state. Let's analyse how walking mechanics work.

A sequence of steps that creates locomotion in animation is called a walk cycle; however, in science, it is referred to as a gait cycle. We will explore this concept further next.

The gait cycle is a series of events that occur during a walk, from the moment one foot touches the surface to the moment it contacts it again, and is often used for clinical assessment and rehabilitation. Using this as an example helps illustrate the process of locomotion during walking (Figure 11.2).

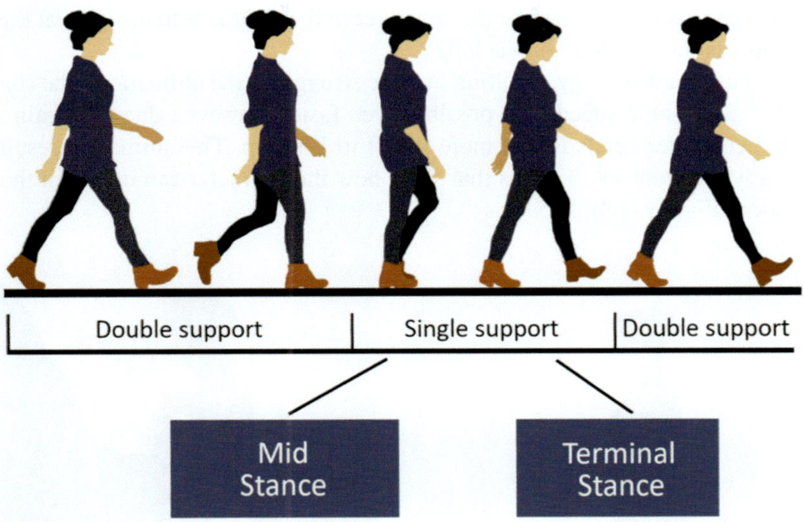

FIGURE 11.2 Image showing the phases of the gait cycle.

We can observe that during the double-support phase, there is initial contact and a loading response. In this phase, the centre of mass remains centred as both legs are in a wide stance for optimal balance and to achieve greater distance. The single support phase involves holding the body weight with a single leg while pushing the body using friction. The mid and terminal stances are the moments when locomotion generates the most thrust, utilizing friction with the surface to propel the body forward in just one leg. Even if the body is not as balanced as in the double support, the mid stance brings the upper body straight above the single leg, which is straight and with the foot flat on the ground, providing full balance and friction. The moment the support leg is behind, due to its push, the terminal stance has the other leg ready for contact, while the upper body is not entirely above both. From there, the swing phase reflects the previous stances, and the process is repeated from the double support once again.

When walking or running, gravity exerts a downward force on our bodies. As we try to resist gravity, we use our muscles and bones to stay upright, along with the laws of motion that help us push against the ground. As long as we keep pushing, we keep moving. However, the body reacts to motion by generating bouncing forces, drag, and overshoot as joints and tissues absorb the energy transferred with each step. This energy is then passed through the body and distributed from the feet to the head in a chain reaction. This chain reaction does not occur all at once, which is why our bodies' movement feels fluid and natural, not mechanical like a robot's, where motion is rigid and uniform. In animation, this chain reaction, known as offset, is crucial to achieving a character's natural movement. It's also important to remember that the distribution of this energy depends on the object's mass, acceleration, and external factors.

By considering the factors mentioned previously, imagine a character navigating a flat surface in the left side image and in an uphill surface in the image on the right. What do you think is needed in order for the character in the right side to navigate at the same acceleration as the character on the left?

More push, more energy, resulting in more struggle in the animation. The character can move at the same speed, and possibly even faster; however, due to terrain differences, the character needs to use more thrust to keep up. The animation results in a significantly different set of poses that show how the character can maintain the same acceleration (Figure 11.3).

FIGURE 11.3 Images of a walk on a flat surface and an uphill surface.

Locomotion involving characters with distinct shapes and masses will also show different results in the animation. A heavier character is much more influenced by gravity, while a lighter one is influenced by air resistance. Not that one force cancels the other, since gravity and air resistance will most likely be acting upon the objects. It is vital to ensure that the characters look realistic and that the forces around them are accurately depicted, allowing the animation to be tackled straightforwardly and directing the energy towards creating impressive, memorable work.

During locomotion, air resistance affects acceleration depending on the object's shape. This resistance causes drag on the body, and the force can increase depending on the mass, flexibility, and the way it is connected to its joint.

Air resistance also causes a drag on the object, resulting in an overshoot when the object eventually comes to a stop.

The effects of gravity are also crucial in determining how locomotion is delivered to the audience. If you have ever had the chance to watch footage of astronauts walking on the surface of the moon, it is interesting to observe how the gravity of a different celestial body can influence the way we move. The astronauts' suits were developed to endure the lack of atmosphere, radiation, and the vacuum of space. With so many layers, the suit weighed an astonishing 200 pounds (90 kg), including the required life support and oxygen system. On the surface of the moon, the weight was reduced to only 30 pounds (13 kg).

On the other hand, even if we could manage to walk on the surface of Jupiter, the astronaut's body would be crushed by the stronger gravitational pull from the giant planet. It is incredible to think about all the environmental factors before starting the animation. I find great joy in conducting research as part of my workflow, and not only do I learn something new, but I also spend less time struggling to complete the first pass of my animation.

Balance is another constant factor; we continuously shift our weight, and the centre of mass constantly changes. We use our arms, upper body, hips, and legs to maintain balance.

Friction and deformation play a role with every step, helping us push forward. The body's weight, along with the increased contact points created by deformation, provides greater grip as we move.

11.2 SWIMMING

Due to its viscosity, water can create buoyancy, which is the ability of objects to stay afloat. Depending on the shape, mass, and size of an object, buoyancy can be achieved effortlessly. It is important to remember that staying afloat does not mean gravity is not acting on an object; rather, some objects can remain buoyant because water is a denser fluid than air, which helps support them. A rubber ball will cut easily through the air if dropped, but it stays afloat when hitting a body of water.

Since water is a denser fluid than air, friction allows us to move from one point to another. When swimming, we push against the water, and our bodies move forward; depending on how we shape our bodies and the energy we exert, we can move much faster and more efficiently.

When moving through the water from one point to another, the body's behaviour differs from what we are used to on the surface. Due to its composition, water behaves differently when an object is partially or fully submerged; even the amount of salt in the water can affect its buoyancy, since salt alters water's density. However, the same set of mechanics is applied to move an object through water.

Consider the locomotion diagram and imagine how you can animate a character moving in water without friction. It is impossible; it would simply sink. If it were an object, it would either sink or remain afloat, relying on the motion of the water. Since locomotion is the ability to move from one place to another, relying on the motion of the water for movement contradicts the very definition of self-generated propulsion.

The same way a fish moves in the water, we do the same, however, with much less proficiency. If the intention is to swim from one point to another, we use the water as a surface to help us with the push. For humans, it is not only a battle to stay afloat; we need to use our entire bodies to keep moving, changing how we position and shape our bodies, and we can achieve different results with swimming locomotion.

I suggest observing swimming competitions to see how athletes move in water. It's fascinating to observe how each technique produces different acceleration as swimmers shape their bodies differently.

Friction and the laws of motion behave slightly differently in water. Because of its composition, water helps objects stay afloat, but it is not as solid as the ground, so more force is needed to move an object when applying friction, pulling, or pushing. By adjusting their body shape in the water, swimmers can go faster or slower and control their buoyancy.

Another important thing to remember is that water also causes body deformation, which you can find more information on in Chapter 9. This effect is minimal at the surface, but as the object moves deeper, deformation has deadly consequences due to pressure. It is important to consider pressure as the character dives deeper underwater.

11.3 FLYING

When creatures are flying, air resistance and lift help counteract gravity. However, without engines or wings to provide continuous thrust, gravity ultimately prevails, and everything that flies within a gravitational field must eventually fall to the ground.

A parachute, for example, can't fly on its own. It must be airborne at a specific altitude to be deployed, and its material, shape, and mass help slow the skydiver's descent through air resistance. The drag force of a parachute is strong enough to reduce the object's terminal velocity. However, gravity remains stronger, and eventually the parachute will reach the surface. A parachute is falling, but still glides, depending on the direction the skydiver decides to pull the strings, or toggles to slightly change the object's shape, and eventually change its path. The function of a parachute is to go from point A, airborne in the sky, to a safer and slower descent on point B, the surface. The object's trajectory is dictated by the skydiver; however, even as the path can be changed, the final destination remains the same.

On the other hand, flying creatures use their legs to propel themselves with a jump. If you observe, there's a fraction of a second where they anticipate, lowering and curving their bodies in a motion that creates an initial push. In animation, this is a great moment to squash the character right before take-off, then stretch it afterwards, which creates a nice sense of fluidity and naturalness.

Flying creatures follow the same pattern of movement. First, there is friction from pushing against the surface, and once they are in the air, their wings move downwards to push the air and stay airborne, following the third law of motion. They can also glide, using air resistance and lift to stay up.

The bigger the bird, the wider its wings must be to lift off and stay in the air. Have you noticed how eagles hunt for relatively large animals, like goats and sheep? They use their wide wings and anatomy to grab other animals and push them off cliffs, letting gravity do the rest. They wouldn't be able to pull off such a feat with different anatomy. Their wide wings help eagles push against the air, carrying extra weight and allowing them to stay in the air for much longer, enabling them to scan the territory for their next prey.

In many movies, comics, or games, we often see flying creatures with very small wings relative to their body size and mass. This can be amusing to support the story, but it is not accurate in real life, nor are characters flying without any mechanism for take-off or equipment to control their trajectory and stay airborne. This is especially unrealistic when characters can, for example, stop a plane from crashing by simply using air resistance. Although this is physically incorrect, it's important to acknowledge a certain level of creative freedom, entertainment, and playability. However, if the goal is to stay true to reality, research and character development should adhere to real-life physics.

Flying locomotion can be seen in many stories and creates a sense of freedom through verticality, allowing the player or audience to explore much more of the world around the characters. It doesn't matter how the character utilizes this form of locomotion, such as magic, superpowers, or technology—whether it launches and keeps them in the air or involves gliding—all of it falls under a flying locomotion system.

11.4 CRAWLING

Crawling animals employ various methods of locomotion, relying on the forces of action and reaction to push against the surface with their bodies. One of the snake's locomotion methods is lateral undulation, characterized by the familiar side-to-side movement. Snakes can also employ concertina locomotion, using their bodies to reach forward, create friction against the surface, and then pull themselves forward in a wavy motion. Afterwards, they anchor their body to the surface to push forward again, forming a loop.

Since some of these creatures lack legs and feet, their bodies provide the primary thrust for movement; it is still considered locomotion, and the diagram remains the same for them.

Referring back to the diagram, friction is the main force driving crawling creatures, and they can move in many ways depending on their mass, shape, composition, and a combination of the laws of motion and friction.

CHAPTER SUMMARY

- Locomotion refers to the basic act of moving from one point to another.
- The ability to move in space, as locomotion, is not limited to walking and running; any motion that transports the subject from point A to point B is considered locomotion.
- As with all animated movements, locomotion needs a purpose and should appear believable, driven by the object's own energy in the intended direction.
- The gait cycle is the equivalent of a walk cycle in animation and describes the period from a foot touching a surface to when it repeats the same action.
- Make sure to understand the surface and angles of the surface on which your character is moving, since these differences will affect the outcome of your animation.
- Friction and push are essential for locomotion to occur.
- Consider the effects of gravity and air resistance when animating locomotion, since each setting and character will behave differently for the story.
- Distinct fluids, like water and air, need to be taken into consideration when animating locomotion, as each has its distinct composition, and the results will affect the character's motion and ability to move.

NOTE

1 Richard Williams, *The Animator's Survival Kit*, Faber & Faber (2001).

Frame of Reference

12

A fundamental part of an animator's job is laying the groundwork for what needs to be delivered in terms of story and performance to the audience at the start of a new project. In other words, the animator's duty is to find ideas or ask the questions regarding the character's emotions, personality, and backstory. It doesn't matter what happens off-screen or the message the animator intends to deliver; if the audience can't see through the camera lens, the message becomes an easter egg for only one person: the animator.

The frame of reference is a crucial aspect of physics and animation and is inherent in everything each spectator sees, depending on factors such as personal experiences, angles, and timing.

The character, camera, and environment all work together to convey a sense of motion to the viewer, and none can fully convey movement without the others.

In physics, the frame of reference can be illustrated by Einstein's train and lightning paradox, also known as the relativity of simultaneity. It tells the story of two observers—one in the middle of a moving train and the other on the ground—who see two lightning strikes from the front and back of the train at the same time. From the perspective of the observer on the ground, both lights flash simultaneously. However, for the passenger on the train, the lightning on the front flashes first because the distance to the front lightning is shorter as they move towards it, compared to the light at the back, which the train observer is moving away from. Neither the passenger nor the outside observer is wrong; their frames of reference simply offer different perspectives on the situation.

You might argue that the observer outside the train is correct, since the lightning flashed at the same time; however, the light paradox shows that simultaneity is relative to each observer's frame of reference.

In animation, the frame of reference is subjective, and similar to the train and lightning paradox, it depends on the observer's perspective. However, in science, the observer's viewpoint is supported by the laws of physics, whereas in animation, it is also influenced by camera framing, characterization, and personal experience.

Picture an animation where a character is running, the camera is following it at the same velocity, and there is no background for motion reference; in other words, you can only see the character, as the camera is our eyes. Who can tell that this character is actually moving in space or just running on a treadmill? The answer is, only the animator who worked on this running cycle knows. If the audience cannot follow, this animation lacks a frame of reference. However, if in this scenario, the animator adds an

DOI: 10.1201/9781003642824-12

As I write this book, the goal of making humanity multiplanetary is more achievable than ever before, and in the future, we may have missions and human landings on Mars; however, as we know, Mars is farther from Earth in relation to the sun, and a trip between the two planets can take nearly a year, depending on their orbits and the cargo involved. Astronauts on the surface of Mars will experience the sunrise almost 5 minutes later than we do on Earth, since the light from the sun takes over 8 minutes to reach us and over 12 minutes to reach Mars.

This is an example of how a five-minute delay in sunrise can significantly influence observers' perspectives, especially when comparing Earth and Mars. However, we don't need to travel far to see a similar effect; this can also be observed with time zones, where one side of the planet experiences day while the other night. Even considering the planet's size, some events can take hours to occur on the opposite side, while others happen almost instantly, like light travelling across the planet.

environment and, instead of moving the character, the environment moves, it appears as if the character is running, and no one can tell otherwise.

This example is an exaggeration, and moving the environment—even if sometimes impossible—will cause significant issues later. However, as the frame of reference indicates, this appears to be a correct scenario visually. But please, do not attempt this in production. I do not want to see you getting in trouble.

A frequently used trick animators use in movies, TV shows, and even some cinematic and gameplay scenes is to break the character's silhouette to support a nice pose, create a specific situation, or hide objects out of the audience's view, since everything outside the camera frame is considered irrelevant for viewers. There are many examples, such as characters picking up or putting away props, broken skeletons, and hyperextensions.

A common way to clarify the frame of reference is to use the camera as the eyes through which the audience sees. Imagine rolling the camera 180°. It doesn't matter what is outside the frame; the reference for the observer is what they can see (Figures 12.1 and 12.2).

Over the years, as technology has evolved, scenes and tricks that were once time-consuming and difficult to achieve have become more realistic and much faster to produce. However, these techniques, once revolutionary, laid the foundation for what software can now do. The substitution splice, one of the earlier techniques in motion pictures, involved stopping the camera during a scene to place or remove actors or objects, then recording again. When applied well, this clever trick would feel seamless to the audience. A character or object disappearing right before the eyes in the early 1900s would seem like magic.

The movie A Trip to the Moon, originally titled Le voyage dans la lune (1902), by the illusionist and filmmaker Georges Méliès, is one of the most important, if not the most important, contributions to visual effects and science fiction in cinema. Using techniques like multiple exposure, dissolves, and substitution spline, the cinematographer

FIGURE 12.1 Zoomed-in framing of two bats.

FIGURE 12.2 Zoomed-out framing of two bats, showing a full perspective.

was able to create this piece and, in a way, bend reality for the audience at the time. It is easy to assume that those behind the camera had a very different experience on set compared to the audience in the theatre.

When planning your animation, focus on what the audience sees on screen; everything else is irrelevant. The storytelling, object and character framing, and post-production must all focus on what the audience will experience. Even if the goal is to leave the audience without answers and to suggest different outcomes, this should also be carefully planned to ensure a great execution.

Writers and artists are partly responsible for delivering the message and setting the tone of a story for the audience, but personal experiences will definitely be a determining factor for each individual watching it.

I often see animators presenting a shot with a finished animation for review, but there's no clear reason why the character behaves that way or what drives its emotion. When the animation has good body mechanics but lacks storytelling, it becomes superficial and generic. The observers—the audience, in this case—will see a good sequence of movement, but won't see the reason why or what is driving the character's intentions.

In some stances, the frame of reference might seem objectively clear to the audience, such as a character design that conveys the idea of a villain; however, focusing solely on one detail, like appearance, cannot make a character truly compelling. This villain requires a background and a clear motivation. Other elements, like camera work, lighting, and music, can also be used to support the idea that the character is a villain.

With all that, can you tell this character is a real villain? Actually, not everyone will agree; some people can still relate to the character's motivation and root for them based on their personal experiences, everything based on their frame of reference.

These are examples of frames of reference, and they're all important for the animator to consider when planning and executing the animation, whether objectively or subjectively. Today, more than ever, information can spread at an enormous speed, and the entire world can access your work. Think about the story you want to tell and the message you want your audience to understand, but also consider the differences that make us human.

CHAPTER SUMMARY

- No matter what happens offscreen or what the animator aims to convey, if the audience can't see through the camera lenses, the message becomes a hidden detail, and the delivery will lack purpose.
- Writers and artists play a role in conveying the message and establishing the story's tone for the audience, but personal experiences will ultimately influence each individual's perception.
- Everything the audience cannot see is irrelevant to the message the animator wants to deliver.

- When considering Einstein's relativity of simultaneity, remember that for each observer, the experience can be viewed from another perspective, leading to a different outcome.
- The lack of background or improper camera angle will possibly affect how the audience reads the message.
- When developing a character, the way it looks is not enough to tell everything about them, when you consider the backstory and the audience's perspective.

Physics of the Principles of Animation

13

My goal in writing this book—sharing years of research and putting it all together into this passion project—has always been to give a small contribution to this art I love so much, and as we begin the final chapter, I wanted to thank you, the reader, for acquiring this book.

I could not ignore the decades of contributions from all artists, writers, and educators who have been spreading their knowledge, mentoring, and preparing new generations of animators every day. Thank you too!

This final chapter is dedicated to all animators who developed the principles of animation and to those who maintain and share this knowledge with the next generations.

In nature, things don't just move without a reason; there must be an intention or external factor for the movement to occur. For that reason, animators should be able to comprehend the mechanics of motion and understand how and why things behave the way they do. This is the essence of being a true master of the craft.

Animation is an illusion of reality, but often requires a touch of exaggeration. It is essential to remember that this is art, and art is inherently subjective; what makes sense to you might not be immediately clear to your audience. However, completely disregarding the laws of physics can lead to serious consequences for the final result. As artists, we need to know when to bend the rules and when to stick to them.

> A good practice I like to follow when working on personal projects is to ask a friend to review my animation; however, if you decide to follow my advice and do the same, keep in mind that this will most likely only work for personal projects, since, as employees in this industry, we tend to work under NDA.[1] Instead, at work, you will have peers who can provide feedback. Throughout your journey in the industry, you will meet with talented animators who will become your friends. It is crucial to understand that you do not have all the answers, and a second pair of eyes will definitely bring some fresh ideas to your work. Being open to feedback will help you grow.
>
> If you're a student, whether you're in a school or with a mentor, ask your teacher and keep asking—we don't mind helping. Also, reach out to your classmates, as they are part of your newly formed network.

DOI: 10.1201/9781003642824-13

At some point in an animator's journey, whether in school or the industry, you will hear about the 12 principles of animation. In the book *The Illusion of Life: Disney Animation*, Frank Thomas and Ollie Johnston compiled the 12 principles from studies of Disney animations spanning the 50 years preceding the book's publication. The goal was to create more believable, interesting animations that follow the laws of physics and realism, with an added touch of creativity. The book was groundbreaking in the industry, and in the years that followed, animators have continued to refer to these principles to create more convincing animations for diverse audiences and media. I highly recommend it for animators of all levels.

Below, I will break down every principle that is related to the laws of physics you read in the previous chapters. Keep in mind that not all principles apply to physics; however, they are equally important for the animation to look appealing to the audience.

13.1 SQUASH AND STRETCH

In physics, squash and stretch refer to Newton's laws of motion, which involve acceleration, mass, and the composition of an object. Depending on these factors, an object can deform, giving the audience a sense of power and elasticity. External factors can also cause characters and objects to squash and stretch, and when both the object's composition and external factors are combined, the object will experience more elasticity.

This deformation can also be observed when anticipation is required to convey more force and power, such as in a jump. To gather more power before a jump, we lower our bodies, creating more distance from the target and using our muscles to slingshot towards it. Breaking down this motion in key poses, your character would go from idle to squat to jump. Can you see the squash and stretch happening? If we keep adding more poses, your character would squash again upon landing and stretch as it settles. In this simple motion, as described, there can be several points where the character squashes and stretches.

This is not limited to body mechanics alone; facial expressions can also deform, squashing and stretching in certain stances. You can have your character's expression deforming on many occasions, like a transition from one expression to another, to avoid a mechanical and linear motion, or to support the body's motion, as in the example above.

If you add facial expressions to the jumping character, you can see a similar transition in squash and stretch from anticipation to the moment the character hits the next pose.

Starting from the idle pose, the face can display a relaxed expression. When transitioning into a squat, the face may shift to a more dynamic expression, such as determination; the eyes can narrow, followed by the eyebrows, and the lips can curl to show more tension. This is the squash happening. When the character jumps, their body stretches along with the expression; their eyes and brows widen, and their mouth slightly opens, with a jaw drop.

This is a general example; depending on the situation, the face can show different expressions; however, it is important to acknowledge that it also deforms as the body does (Figure 13.1).

FIGURE 13.1 Image of a person jumping from one platform to another.

It is important to consider that squash and stretch are directly related to deformation, as discussed in Chapter 9.

Deformation from squash and stretch is based on the object's composition, the force applied, and, in some cases, the reaction force. The last of which occurs when the shape of object A is affected by the opposing force exerted by object B. Can you think of any similar phenomenon that occurs when two objects interact with each other in the same way? If your answer was the third law of motion, discussed in Chapter 5, you are correct.

Deformation can also occur due to gravity. The higher the fall, the greater the deformation from the reaction force, combined with the object's composition, mass, and external force applied onto it. Depending on the object's composition, gravity alone can stretch an object. In the bouncing ball exercise, which is a great way to understand squash and stretch, you may have seen that deformation occurs as the ball falls towards the ground, creating a stretched shape. During this moment, the stretching deformation follows its trajectory, as shown in Figure 13.2. However, when the ball hits the surface, its energy is redirected in all directions except along its original trajectory, because the surface opposes the object's motion. It is essential to remember that, regardless of how much the object squashes and stretches, its mass remains unchanged; it is only redistributed to the areas of less resistance.

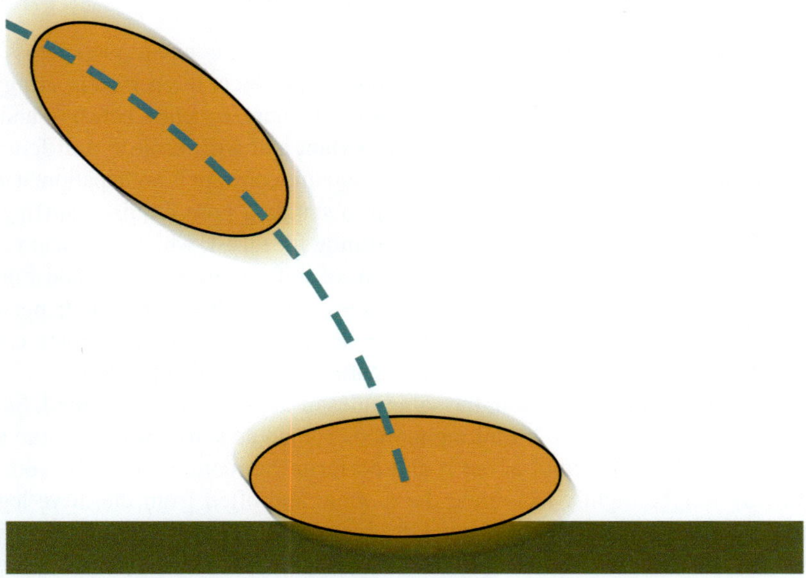

FIGURE 13.2 Image of a ball falling because of gravity and deforming due to the reaction force.

Regarding action and reaction, the response of the object and its deformation will be relative to the force applied to it.

All these factors can be applied together or independently for squash and stretch. Before starting the animation, the animator should ask about the external factors and determine the object's weight and composition. Planning the animation is the first step to completing it efficiently.

13.2 ANTICIPATION

In animation, you may have heard that anticipation gives the audience time to understand what is about to happen from one pose to the next, bringing naturalness to the character's motion and making it less mechanical. However, in physics, there is a more fundamental answer to why anticipation occurs.

In nature, anticipation is essentially a weight shift that provides humans and animals with the balance needed to support the following action. We are constantly shifting our weight as we move; at any moment, more weight can be on one leg than the other. The same happens when sitting. The weight can be more on one side than the other, sometimes even balancing on the arms, torso, or anything in contact with the other object. So, you can imagine what it's like when we transition from a sitting to a standing pose. If you can, try it now. From a relaxed sitting position, stand up and observe how anticipation feels in your situation.

Every scenario is different, especially when considering compensation across limbs due to differences in strength, injuries, or genetics. The object the person is sitting on is also crucial, since there are many types and styles of chairs, couches, benches, and other surfaces encountered. All these factors are important and will result in a different outcome for an animation. However, one thing that remains constant is anticipation; it always occurs. In short, transitioning from a sitting to a standing pose requires shifting body weight to find balance first. The next step is pushing for thrust, which will help perform the action with the gathered energy. These actions of shifting the weight and pushing give the observer the time to understand, and sometimes predict what is about to happen.

It is essential to understand that, during anticipation, other principles can and should overlap with it to make the animation natural, fluid, and appealing.

When considering locomotion, the same rules of anticipation are applied. Suppose you want to go from an idle to a walking motion. You could start a walk without anticipation, but if you do not think about it and perform the motion naturally, your body will shift its weight slightly to initiate the motion, and often from the drive leg. The reason this happens—and why it is not just about motion without anticipation, which feels mechanical and unnatural—is that we not only seek balance, which is a key part of anticipation, but also gather more power to initiate the motion.

For example, a boxer drops the body and slightly leans forward before delivering an uppercut, using the opposite arm to maintain balance. Additionally, the arms are positioned wide enough to provide stability, enabling a stance that supports anticipation. This involves crouching, leaning the torso, bringing the arm back to gain distance, and, consequently, achieving more acceleration for an effective strike (Figure 13.3).

FIGURE 13.3 Image capturing a boxer's anticipation for an uppercut.

Another example comes from a sword master who is about to strike a target. Without anticipation, it is possible to cause damage; however, by maintaining distance from the target and keeping balance, the momentum generated will be greater than when striking without anticipation. Engaging their entire body in the motion opposite to the strike not only creates spacing and anticipation for the audience to understand what is about to happen, but also allows the animator to play with poses, aiming to achieve a smooth line of action for the character, or even some squash and stretch. As you can observe, the sword master arches their body backwards, shifting their centre of mass before delivering the strike; at this point, the body will arch in the opposite direction, as a bow fully drawn with an arrow. The next motion releases the tension, causing the strong slashing (Figure 13.4).

FIGURE 13.4 Image of a sword master striking bamboo.

As you can observe, anticipation comes with a weight shift to maintain balance. Without it, the following motion would not be as powerful and direct as expected. For either strong or subtle motion, it is natural to see anticipation, and it always comes with a certain level of balance for the character.

By nature, humans tend to look for less effort in motion; in some instances, the anticipation can be very subtle. It is important to remember that simple, subtle animation does not necessarily mean a bad animation, as long as you apply elements that make it natural and interesting, along with strong storytelling.

Anticipation is not limited to punches or sword slashes; it is in everything, even if discreet, and it plays an important role not only in animation but also in physics.

13.3 OVERLAPPING ACTION AND FOLLOW-THROUGH

When an object initiates its motion, the energy isn't spread out all at once through it. Instead, the area where the energy is concentrated initiates the motion, and then the energy spreads to its loose and attached segments, like a chain reaction. In other words, any part of the object that is not completely attached to the driving object will have the energy ripple through it with a delay, causing drag and overshoot reaction.

This delayed response depends on the acceleration, mass, and composition of all the objects. During this process, some of the laws, forces, and principles of physics discussed in this book are applied. Overlap and follow-through are the animation terms used to explain this concept.

In short, this principle concerns the response of objects to a driving force, and a good example is a simple pendulum in motion.

As we know from Newton's first law of motion, an object at rest tends to stay at rest, so the motion must be initiated either by the object itself or by external forces. In Figure 13.5, the driving force is the creature's body driving the tail. However, it can be many other things, like: A human head driving the hair or the part of the suit where a super hero's cape is attached.

FIGURE 13.5 Overlap of a creature's tail.

For the sake of this example, I will refrain from adding more principles to avoid confusion.

Imagine a creature in motion with a tail. As discussed, when the character runs, the energy in their body does not originate from the tail; it comes from the hips, legs, and other parts of the body. This energy, distributed throughout the body, is essential for pushing. Some body parts of this animal, like the tail and ears, can be controlled, but are not the source of energy to initiate a run, for example. These areas will, in fact, react to the motion with a delay since they are dragged and at the same time carry enough weight to resist the motion, as it happens with the pendulum. When the tail reacts to the pull, the character is already in motion, resulting in overlapping action. The same applies when the character stops: The delay present during acceleration also occurs during deceleration.

When animating, many animators, including myself, tend to avoid adding overlap during the character's blocking stage. For the first pass, we aim to capture the timing, pose, and overall motion and feeling from the character, and details like overlap and follow-through can cause confusion when working with a complex character. Instead of spending too much time on overlapping and follow-through, focus on strong poses and timing. This also helps you share your animation sooner for feedback and ensures you're on the right track. Nobody wants to spend excessive time on every small detail, only to find that when feedback arrives, the vision is unclear and many fundamental errors—which could have been easily addressed in the first pass—must be fixed later, leading to a backlog and unnecessary extra work.

Figure 13.6 shows how the force originates in the shoulder and ripples through the arm to the wrist. As you can see, the shoulder initiates the movement by driving and rotating first. The initial delayed motion occurs at the elbow, as it is the nearest joint to the shoulder, and from there, the energy transfers to the wrist and fingers. This is just a small example, and this motion also ripples throughout the rest of the body, causing overshoot, overlap, and offset because the energy does not move all at once.

FIGURE 13.6 Image showing the transfer of energy between the joints during arm movement.

13.4 EASE IN, EASE OUT

Ease in and out, also known as slow in and slow out, is directly linked to Newton's laws of motion. Still, it is also influenced significantly by human psychology and body mechanics.

Inertia causes a motion to start slowly, as the body resists a change in its state of rest. When initiating motion, acceleration must be gradual, taking both force and mass into account.

When it comes to slowing down or easing out, this is more about human behaviour than physics, as we tend to decelerate to avoid injuries from sudden stops or collisions. As we age, we become more controlled in our movements to reduce the risk of injury. Of course, there is a biological reason for senior citizens to move slowly or carefully; however, when observing children and adults, it is easy to see who controls their movements most to avoid breaking something or getting injured.

When we initiate an action, such as reaching for a cup of water, we first send a signal from our brain to our body. The moment our arms receive the message, we prepare our hands to wrap around the cup; unconsciously, we analyse the material so we can determine how tightly to grip it, allowing us to lift it for a sip without holding it too tightly, thereby avoiding breaking the object and suffering potential injuries. For an action like reaching for a glass and bringing it to the mouth, the body motion will have several moments of slow ins and slow outs. However, between these moments, once the hand is in motion towards the glass, we increase speed once we have built enough force and analysed the safe distance from the body and the object.

It is essential to understand that, in certain situations, ease in will occur, but ease out should not, as adding it would make the animation appear unrealistic.

I often observe this with entry-level animators working with 3D software: Just before a significant impact—such as a strike, landing, or crash—the animation suddenly loses acceleration where it should not. This occurs because of a lack of experience: The software applies a standard tangent with ease-ins and ease-outs, since that typically happens naturally. The software lacks a way to specify when certain moments should be fast or slow; it's therefore up to the animator to address this.

Think of a combat animation where a character throws a punch. At the moment of contact, there is no loss of acceleration, which makes the impact powerful. However, at the start, there is a slight easing as the body needs to establish balance for a strong stance—or, as we know in animation, anticipation, as seen previously. After that, the energy is distributed, originating from the friction of the feet, the rotation of the hips and torso, the shoulders, and finally the arm. All the body mass and energy are transferred from the anticipation pose to the moment of contact, resulting in gradual acceleration. If the punch slows down before contact, the impact will not be as strong, and very little damage will be inflicted. Keep in mind that when a character transitions from a punch pose to another, such as an idle pose, the ease-out should be considered, as it is a natural response as the character settles (Figure 13.7).

The same occurs when we land or fall; at the moment of contact, we are at maximum speed as the body reaches terminal velocity. Keep in mind that terminal velocity

FIGURE 13.7 Ease in during a punch.

occurs when there is enough distance from the surface; it does not happen when we jump off a chair, for example. Regardless, the acceleration is constant until the moment of contact with the surface.

The bouncing ball exercise, which I personally recommend to any aspiring animator, demonstrates this very simply and can be applied to almost anything.

Since the ball has no legs or any other means of propulsion, the best approach is to start from a distance above the surface; this helps add credibility to the animation. When the ball is dropped, it appears to remain in the air for a short time, as the descent starts slowly. As the object falls, the rate increases, and the tendency is to gain speed until it touches the surface. At the moment of contact, there is no gradual deceleration; it will hit at the maximum speed (Figure 13.8).

Unlike a ball, humans can use their legs to push against the ground and propel themselves into the air through jumping. During this process, the ease in happens as we lower our bodies, gathering energy to push. However, as we lose contact with the surface, we reach maximum speed until gravity pulls us down, starting from the moment we hang, and eventually land at the maximum speed.

13.5 ARCS

Arcs are among the most unforgiving principles when not applied correctly, and the consequences can not only break the laws of physics but also alter the character's entire character and trajectory. It is surprisingly common that, in my regular reviews, I come across animations with strong poses and great potential, yet broken arcs. I assume that some animators focus so much on poses and other principles that they end up ignoring

FIGURE 13.8 Image comparing a person and a ball landing.

arcs in the process. Or perhaps there is a lack of polish and a rush to deliver the animation, causing the animator to miss cleaning up the arcs. Regardless, since arcs are inherent in almost everything, ignoring them can lead to significant issues in the animation (Figure 13.9).

Most things in nature follow an arc-shaped trajectory, but the reasons for this can stem from many factors. Humans and animals move through a coordinated effort of muscles and nerves, but the skeleton provides the structure and frame for the motion. The joints in our skeleton are the points where movement occurs, as previously discussed in Chapter 10. Since bones cannot change their shape, and arcs occurs due to the pivot at the joints, the natural motion of our body follows an arc for every movement, much like a pendulum. It is easier to observe the arc trajectory in motion when discussing endoskeletons like ours.

A common mistake I notice is that, instead of rotating the shoulders during elevation—also known as a shrug—animators translate it, moving the shoulder up, which deforms and breaks the character. This issue is most visible, but not limited to, characters wearing shoulder pads or designed with broad shoulders.

Shoulder elevation occurs when the trapezius and levator scapulae contract, causing the clavicle—also known as the shoulder blade—to move. The clavicle, which supports this motion, pivots on the sternum as these muscles engage to elevate the shoulder.

FIGURE 13.9 Image of the human body moving along an arc path.

When some animators translate the shoulders rather than creating a natural pose and motion, the character feels broken and overly flexible. In some cases, applying translation to the shoulder can help the animator craft a more appealing pose; however, it is essential to ensure the character's volume stays within its limits. Figure 13.10 shows a shoulder rotation during its elevation motion. If, instead of rotation, the upward translation is applied, the clavicle bone would stretch, deforming the shoulder in the process.

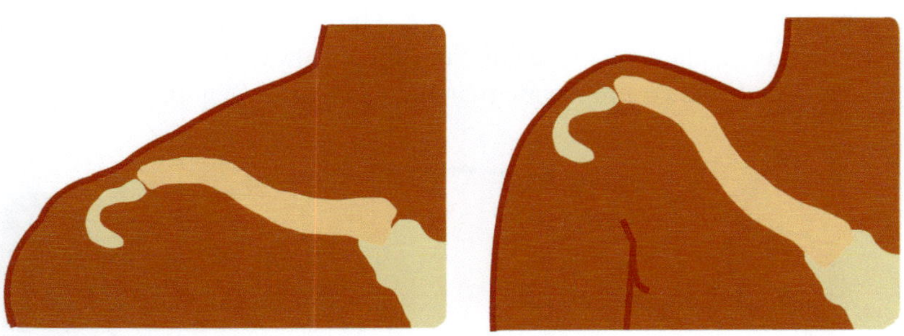

FIGURE 13.10 Example of shoulder raise.

The shoulders are just one example of the range of motion the human body can achieve through rotation. It's important to remember that when you animate, the body is limited by its skeleton, and every single bone that can move does so because it pivots with other bones. However, when animating and aiming for the best delivery, breaking the character a little can lead to impressive animations, as long as it supports the flow and clarity in the camera view or pushes the animation and poses for more appealing results outside the view, for example, a character with their hands behind their back. In some games, these can be great opportunities to hide a prop in a single frame, making it disappear—like creating the illusion of putting a phone in a pocket.

When objects are thrown or projected into the air, such as during a jump, they always have an arc-shaped trajectory due to projectile motion and the force of gravity, as seen in Chapters 1 and 7. It is important to remember that once in motion, the arc trajectory can be interrupted only by an external force acting on the object (Figure 13.11).

FIGURE 13.11 Image of a rabbit leaping in an arc.

Inexperienced animators often compensate for action scenes—such as parkour performances or takedowns—by adding extra keyframes in animation software. This creates an irregular trajectory, breaking the animation's sense of naturalness and smoothness. When viewed by an untrained eye, a broken trajectory might feel off even if said viewer can't explain why. The animator should always use available tools to follow the correct path and ensure the arc is smooth and clean (Figure 13.12).

FIGURE 13.12 Image of a bowman shooting an arrow upwards along an arc trajectory.

For creatures with exoskeletons, such as ants and scorpions, or hydrostatic skeletons, like earthworms and octopuses, the arc can be more subtle and, at times, erratic. However, they also follow the same trajectory if you observe.

13.6 TIMING

As Albert Einstein once said, "Time is relative."[2] That said, if you decide or accidentally animate a character moving very slowly, and someone gives feedback saying the timing is off, you could argue that the character is near a black hole, and whoever is providing the feedback is the stationary observer far away. You might get some laughs, but not a job.

In animation, understanding and delivering proper timing is one of the most critical aspects of our work. An animation with poor timing can break the immersion and flow. No matter how good the story is, when the timing is off, everything feels off.

Timing is all about understanding the story being told and the laws of physics acting on the world and everything else that resides there. The storyteller should know the setting and environment, the effects of gravity, and the composition of things in this world. With those answers in mind, the story and animation should be built after careful research so that everything there feels like it belongs in the world created.

There is a misconception that video game animations are fast, and I honestly beg to differ: While game animation, or gameplay more specifically, can indeed be faster to aim for responsiveness and a more engaging experience for the player, not all games need to be fast. This really depends on the story and design choices.

Breaking some of the laws of physics to create a playable and fun game or to enhance and support storytelling in a movie is acceptable, as long as this is not done in every animation and is done carefully. In fact, if you think of any stylized animated movie or show that breaks the laws of timing, the entire world and characters tend to adopt the style, making the animation feel normal, and anything else based in reality would seem strange to the viewer. It all depends on how the elements connect in the story.

With all that said, I encourage you to use references and observe how things move in real life to deepen your understanding of timing. Remember that in nature, most things don't always move at the same pace. The animator needs to be able to play with the beats in the story and understand when the animation should be slower or faster.

Principles like exaggeration, solid drawing, appeal, staging, straight-ahead action, pose-to-pose, and secondary action don't directly apply to the physics of animation. However, they are equally essential to consider when animating anything. To tell a compelling story and create engaging animation, be mindful and ensure you explore and apply all the principles.

CHAPTER SUMMARY

- While art is subjective and limiting creativity is not the aim, neglecting the fundamentals of reality and physics can negatively affect the animation, as the audience needs a hint of realism to connect with.
- Do not underestimate the power of feedback; having trusted people around to offer opinions and suggestions for improvement will help you achieve the best results. However, ultimately, this is your animation, and it's important to know how much you can change before losing your original idea.
- Squash and Stretch is a result of gravity, deformation, and Newton's laws of motion, and it is essential to consider the subject's composition and environment to achieve the best results in the animation.
- Squash and Stretch give the audience a sense of naturalness and elasticity.
- Anticipation is a moment for the audience to understand what is about to happen and how powerful the following action will be, through a combination of weight shift, spacing, and timing.
- Follow-Through and Overlapping Action refer to the chain reaction from an object's driving force, as the energy is distributed with a delay to the object's attached or loose segments.
- Inertia is crucial for follow-through and overlap to occur, as the law states, an object at rest tends to stay at rest, and an object in motion tends to stay in motion, unless acted upon by an external force.
- The law of inertia also affects ease in and ease out, as objects tend to resist their state of rest and motion.
- As ease in can be observed in almost anything, ease out is more frequently seen when there is a sudden interruption in an object's motion, such as an uncontrolled landing or crash.
- Arcs occur in nearly everything in nature because bones pivot at joints or follow a path. Forces such as gravity and air resistance act on the object to trace the arc trajectory.
- Understand the world you've created and its natural influences to achieve proper and natural timing in the animation.

NOTES

1 NDA: Non-disclosure Agreement.
2 Albert Einstein, *Theory of Special Relativity* (1905).

Index

L

M

N

O

P

R

S

T

U

V

W

For Product Safety Concerns and Information please contact our EU representative GPSR@taylorandfrancis.com Taylor & Francis Verlag GmbH, Kaufingerstraße 24, 80331 München, Germany